The British
Veterinary
Association

GUIDE TO
DOG
CARE

The British Veterinary Association

GUIDE TO DOG CARE

DAVID TAYLOR
B.V.M.S., F.R.C.V.S.

DORLING KINDERSLEY LONDON

First published in Great Britain in 1989
by Dorling Kindersley Limited,
9 Henrietta Street, London WC2E 8PS

This book is compiled from material previously
published in *You and Your Dog* by David Taylor

British Library Cataloguing in Publication Data
Taylor, David *1934-*
   The British Veterinary Association guide to dog care.
   1. Pets: Dogs. Care
   I. Title
   636.7'083

   ISBN 0-86318-403-0

Produced by Mandarin Offset in Hong Kong

CONTENTS

INTRODUCTION

"Who loves me will love my dog also", are the immortal words of St Bernard, a twelfth century dog-lover. Today, well over a hundred different breeds are kept as pets in Britain. There are countless reasons why dogs are among the most rewarding pets and the most faithful of "family friends". They are sociable animals and love human company. Children and elderly people, probably those with the most free time, are likely to be the most constant companions to their dogs and best able to build up a special relationship with them.

A dog has so much to give if treated with care and common sense. Its protective instincts are naturally strong, and the desire to guard things and keep them safe extends to a dog's owner and family and their house and garden.

A friendly dog is interested in all your family activities and loves to be at the centre of things. Your dog is your greatest fan and its loyalty is unquestioning. If you and your family respect your dog and its needs, it will respect you.

This books aims to guide you through the important elements of dog ownership. It is divided into three chapters: *Caring For Your Dog, Feeding,* and *Health Care.* The first includes everything you need to know about choosing a dog, adapting your house and garden safely for a new dog or puppy, equipment you need, handling a dog, play and exercise, travelling, toilet training, obedience training and grooming. The dog comes in an amazing range of types and sizes, so choosing the right pet requires care and forethought. You may like the look of a particular breed, but it is important to make sure you can cope with all its needs in terms of day-to-day care. Welcoming an adult dog into your home calls for just as much consideration as for a puppy, and you must do your best to make sure your new pet feels happy.

Training is covered in clear step-by-step sequences showing the right way to handle your dog during obedience training. By taking the trouble to train your pet, you're doing both of you a good turn, and helping it to fit in more easily with your own lifestyle. Thorough, careful grooming contributes to your dog's good health and well-being. Find out how to use grooming tools in the right way and how to deal with different types of coat.

Feeding is dealt with in the second chapter. Understanding which components make up a balanced canine diet helps you to feed your dog the right food in the correct amounts. There's useful information on feeding bowls, feeding times, giving water and "eating between meals". The third chapter is devoted to a comprehensive survey of your dog's body and the problems that can occur within it. Recognizing the signs that all is not well is the key to prompt and successful treatment, so use the quick-diagnosis charts to point you in the right direction. Selections on each system or section of the dog's body are accompanied by boxes on common symptoms, plus practical instructions on treatment techniques you can carry out at home. Both simple and serious conditions and diseases are identified, and their treatment and prevention explained. Caring for elderly and ill dogs at home is covered, as well as taking a sick animal to the vet. Properly practised, first aid can be a lifesaver. Clear diagrams and checklists show you how to deal with a whole range of emergencies.

The saying "it's a dog's life" has a strongly pejorative ring to it. After dipping into this book and, I hope, enjoying what it has to offer, I trust the words will take on for you a more positive and delightful meaning.

An obedient pet
Show younger members of the family how to reinforce your dog's training exercises.
Careful training is one of the most important aspects of life with your dog.

CARING FOR
YOUR DOG

There are several decisions to be made when choosing
a dog, and this chapter will help you make them.
Welcoming a puppy or adult dog into your home
involves a new set of responsibilities, and you should
be as good a companion to your dog as it is to you.
Your reward for careful handling and training will be
a sociable, obedient pet you'll be proud to be seen out
and about with. Responsible ownership means
choosing the right equipment. Follow the advice on
choosing and using collars, leads, beds, food and
water bowls, toys and grooming equipment for your
dog. Helpful checklists help you make sure your
house and garden are safe for the new arrival.
Valuable pages on travelling, exercise, toilet and
obedience training and grooming show you the best
approach to all these aspects of your dog's life.

Choosing a dog

Man has a long-standing link with dogs – an extension of the basic attachment that maintains contact between people. Human relationships are based on "social signals" – facial expression, eye and voice contact, time spent together, mutual dependancy and responsibility, the reassurance of touch. These behavioural signals are also seen between people and pets.

Why have a dog?

Dogs seek out people and take obvious pleasure in their company. They often fulfil a childlike role and are dependent on their owners throughout their life. This dependancy works both ways. The psychological value of stroking a dog is well-known to doctors – it reduces stress and lowers blood pressure. Your dog is part of your family – friend, protector, companion, comforter, entertainer. You'll wonder how you ever managed without it.

What age of dog?

This is one of the first decisions you should make. Of course, a puppy is delightful, especially if you've got children, but there may be reasons why an older dog is more appropriate.

If you're looking for a good companion and you'd like to take it out and about with you right from the start, a young adult dog may suit you best. Elderly people can find a puppy a strain, but may be able to give a good home to a displaced older dog.

Puppies

If you choose a puppy, there should be someone at home all day, or periodically throughout the day. You must spend time with a puppy, both to develop a good relationship with it and to give it the chance to become properly house-trained. Taking a young puppy away from its mother is quite a serious upset; frequent separations from you can cause problems.

Pedigree dogs come in all shapes and sizes, as this happy, healthy collection shows.

Older dogs

If you choose an older dog, make sure it is house-trained – a dog that has been kennelled for a long time may not be. Find out exactly why the dog needs a home – it could be nervous, aggressive or dirty around the house. You must be prepared to be patient with the dog. Again, don't leave it alone for too long.

What size of dog?

Size is an important consideration. Large dogs may be good intruder deterrents, but could lead to a visit from the bank manager instead! Large breeds are expensive both to buy and to feed. Once grown up, they need a great deal of exercise. They aren't suited to city centres, particularly houses or flats with small gardens. Walking a dog late at night can be risky in a city and your initial resolve to take it out regularly could weaken.

Small children can be knocked over by big, bouncy puppies, and elderly people often find large breeds a handful. But most giant breeds are as gentle as they are large and, once adult, usually careful with children.

Small and toy breeds need far less exercise – they'll virtually exercise themselves in a garden, particularly if two are kept together. Take care with toy dogs – young children can accidentally hurt them seriously.

What kind of dog?

Dogs and bitches both have pros and cons. Bitches are easier to train and more likely to form a solid attachment to their owner. However, their twice-yearly "heat" can mean a messy discharge and problems with dogs.

Many people think that dogs have more character. Their more dominant nature can make them harder to train and more likely to challenge human authority. They will roam in search of bitches if one is on heat locally. Both sexes can be surgically neutered, but there should always be a valid reason.

Pedigree or mongrel?

Once you know which breed you want, choosing a pedigree dog means you know about its size, temperament, feeding, exercise and grooming needs. Mongrels, although not as predictable, have many points in their favour. Most are attractive and energetic. They're less afflicted by inherited diseases and seem to avoid some common ailments.

Choosing a puppy

When choosing a puppy from a litter, there are several points to look for regarding health and suitability as a pet. Watch the litter playing to assess character. A healthy puppy has:
- Bright and alert eyes with no discharges or cataracts.
- Clean skin and ears.
- Well-formed faeces.
- Correctly aligned teeth.
- Well-proportioned body – not fat.

A special relationship
Your new puppy will soon come to rely on you, not just for food, but also for affection and companionship – things it can give you, too.

Your dog's new home

The question of when a puppy should move to its new home causes more problems than any other. There can be psychological conflicts between a caring breeder parting with a litter of puppies and a new owner eager to acquire one of them. A breeder may even delay selling a particular puppy because it has show potential and could command a higher price later, or even to be too good to sell.

For getting to know its new family, six to seven weeks is the best time to move a puppy. From this age, the more human contact it experiences, the better its temperament will be. Although there are no hard and fast rules, smaller, more insecure breeds and puppies going to noisy homes with very young children are often best left until ten weeks. Allow an adult dog to settle quietly into its new home.

MAKING YOUR HOUSE AND GARDEN SAFE

Houses are designed for people and can contain hidden hazards for dogs, particularly young puppies. In the house, watch out for any exposed electric flex in places where it can be chewed, especially in out-of-sight corners. Make sure the puppy can't fall down stairs or stair-wells by putting up guards. Although you may feel a little silly, it is well worth going round every room in the house on all-

fours, to see exactly what is within reach of an inquisitive, playful puppy!

Examine the garden to make sure your puppy or dog can't get out. A garden gate is often a weak spot – cover it with wire netting to make it secure. With a puppy, you must feel quite sure that no dogs can get in from outside before it has had all its vaccinations. If possible, fence off a section of the garden where you can

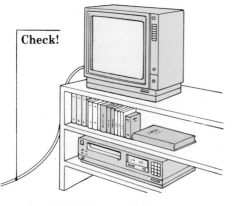

Check!

Check the house
- Exposed electric flex
- Stairs and stair-wells
- Any projections which could catch on the puppy's collar and strangle it
- Check rooms on all-fours

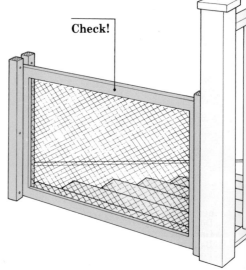

Check!

Equipment

If you're acquiring a new dog or puppy, there is certain equipment you need to ensure its happiness and safety in your home. This includes:

- Bed and bedding (see p.14)
- Food and water bowls (see p.35)
- Suitable diet (see pp.32–7)
- Collar, lead and identity tag (see p.15)
- Grooming equipment (see p.26)
- Toys (see p.17)
- Travelling box (small dogs, see p.18)
- First aid kit (see p.88).

safely leave the puppy for short periods; it can also use this run as a toilet area.

Check your garage and garden sheds for items that could fall on the puppy and make sure that no dangerous poisons like weedkiller or slug and rat baits have been left around. Finally, put up guards to protect the puppy from any other garden hazards such as pools, ponds and steep drops at the edges of patios or lawns.

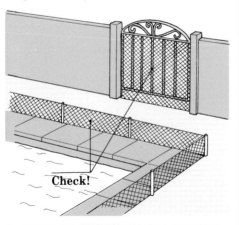

Check!

Check the garden
- Dog-proof boundaries, especially gates
- Garage and sheds
- Baits and poisons
- Ponds and steep drops

The puppy's bed

A bed of its own makes a very important contribution to a puppy's sense of security in its new home. It will certainly miss its mother, brothers and sisters and previous home so will benefit from having its own "territory". The first bed doesn't have to be elaborate – a cardboard box with the front cut down provides a good start. The only bedding needed is newspaper with a folded blanket on top. Once the teething stage is over and the puppy chewing less, you can provide a sturdier bed (see p.14).

Puppy food and water bowls

Your puppy needs separate bowls for food and water. When deciding where to put them, remember that the water should be available at all times, so choose an out-of-the-way place with an impervious surface. Place the bowls on newspaper to keep any stray food tidy; when the puppy is past the chewing stage, you can place them on a plastic wipe-down mat.

The first night

Just before bedtime, give the dog or puppy an opportunity to relieve itself. Almost inevitably, your first few nights' sleep will be disturbed. A homesick dog will be upset at night when you and your family disappear to bed and will probably cry. There are two approaches to this. You can ignore the crying until the animal settles down. Never punish it for crying – this only increases its misery. After a quiet night, praise your puppy or dog. The alternative is to place a pen in the bedroom of one of the family and let it sleep there for a couple of weeks. This can cause problems in itself, since children especially tend to weaken your resolve to keep your pet out of bedrooms and off beds.

Dog beds

A bed or kennel is an important part of your dog's surroundings and provides it with its own territory, refuge and "reference point". Every dog needs its own place to sleep; some may also benefit from having a kennel and perhaps an outdoor pen.

A bed for your dog

A cardboard box is fine for a growing, teething puppy, and easily replaced if soiled or damaged. As the puppy grows up, you'll probably decide to buy it a proper bed or basket.

You can buy dog beds at most pet shops, although owners of giant breeds may need to spend time finding a suitable one. Choose one that will only leave a little space round your dog when it is fully grown, while allowing for bedding.

Bedding

Anything soft and warm – old towels, jumpers or blankets – is ideal. Wash them regularly. You can also place a bean bag in the bed or basket – line the bed with newspaper first.

Cleaning the bed

Dogs will happily sleep on beds which smell (to us) incredibly "doggy". This does little to enhance their personal freshness. You should wash bed and bedding regularly, every time you bath the dog and between-times as well. Scrub the bed or basket with a non-toxic disinfectant diluted with hot water.

Where to put the bed

Place your dog's bed in a secluded, draught-free part of the house.

TYPES OF BED

Dog beds come in a wide range of sizes and shapes. **Wicker baskets** are traditional and popular; their friendly creaking may reassure a dog. However, they're hard to clean and large pieces can be chewed off and swallowed – watch this. **Plastic beds** are resilient and suitable for dogs that seem to be reassured by chewing their bed. Some small breeds like the "igloo" type sold for cats – these surround the animal snugly and securely. **Bean bags** make a comfortable and self-contained bed.

Igloo-type for small dogs

Wicker basket

Rigid plastic bed

Collars and leads

Pet shops stock a bewildering array of collars and leads. In general, choice depends on preference, but there are a few points to watch.

Choosing a lead

Leads are usually made of rope, leather, chain or nylon. For large breeds, choose a strong lead, either a stout leather one or the chain sort with a leather handle. Badly trained dogs that chew their leads also need chains. Nylon leads are easy to wash and lightweight, so they're handy to put in your pocket.

It is possible to buy a lead on a rewinding spool, extending to 4.5m or 6m. Although the lead is compact to hold, it lets the dog explore while you remain in control.

Choosing a collar

Most collars for dogs are leather, but chain and nylon ones are also available. A leather collar 12 mm wide is suitable for most dogs; larger breeds will need 2.5–4 cm width.

Several countries require a dog to wear an identity tag on its collar in case of loss or accident; several types are available.

A puppy's first collar

Even though a puppy isn't allowed out on the streets until after its course of vaccinations, it is a good idea to accustom it to collars and leads.

POINTS OF SAFETY

When giving a puppy its first collar:
- Don't fasten the collar too tightly; you should be able to slide several fingers underneath it
- Don't use a choke chain on a young puppy – you could damage its neck
- Don't leave anything projecting on which the puppy could catch the collar and accidentally hang itself

USING A CHOKE CHAIN COLLAR

A choke chain (or check chain) is a training aid and should *not* be worn all the time. It is meant to control a dog while out walking or during training. If worn continually, there's more risk of it catching things. Always have the dog on your left-hand side. It is important to put the collar on the right way round, so that the weight of the chain loosens the loop after the collar has checked the dog.

From the ring, the chain should pass in front of the dog's neck, round the neck and back through the ring to the lead.

Handling a dog

When dealing with a friendly dog that already knows you, follow these general guidelines:
● Be gentle but firm at all times
● Speak in a reassuring voice
● Don't startle the dog
● Don't tease the dog or take advantage of its friendly nature

A responsible dog owner should have the trust of his dog and should be able to hold it still, pick it up or carry it without any panic or aggression. The degree of holding and cuddling that dogs will tolerate varies – it depends partly on temperament, partly on owner conditioning. Most dogs revel in it, given the opportunity.

However, it is also important to teach your dog to accept physical restraint from you. Train it by restraining it for very short periods from puppyhood so that it doesn't see your gesture as a threat. You'll need to restrain it at the vet's (see p.82).

HANDLING A STRANGE DOG

If you encounter a strange dog, perhaps in an enclosed space, it may show aggression, growling or baring its teeth. There are a few things to remember in this situation:
● Speak in a calm, firm voice
● Don't make any sudden moves. If the dog shows any aggression, keep still
● Don't challenge the dog by staring
● If all is well, offer a clenched fist to be sniffed (fingers are vulnerable)
● Don't crouch by the dog unless you know it is safe. Stoop from the waist so you can straighten to avoid bites
● If you're uncertain, keep your distance. Don't threaten the dog or block its exit path
● Look around for an object for self-defence if this should prove necessary, but don't show it to the dog
● When you leave, invite the dog to come too; don't make it look like a retreat

PICKING UP A DOG

If you need to pick up or carry a dog, talk to it first so that it is not surprised to be handled. If you're alone and you're in any doubt about the dog's temperament, muzzle it first (see p.89).

To pick up a small dog, place one hand under its chest. Use the other to support its rear end, the way you'd lift a cat.

To lift a larger dog, place one hand or arm under its chest in front of its forelegs and one under its hind legs. Bend your knees before lifting the dog rather than bending from the waist. It often helps to have a second person gently holding the dog's head and talking to it. This stops it panicking and turning to bite your face.

The right way to pick up a dog
Whatever the size of dog, make sure that its front and rear ends are both supported.

Play and exercise

Every dog needs regular exercise to keep it fit and healthy. Dogs which don't have enough exercise become obese. Generally, your dog will take as much exercise as you want to take yourself. However, if you're very athletic and enjoy hill-walking or long-distance jogs, your dog will need to build up to this gradually.

Avoiding over-exercise

Large dogs, particularly giant breeds, should never be over-exercised before they're 12 months old. Bones and muscles are still developing and too much exercise in puppyhood can cause long-term problems. It isn't easy to say exactly how much exercise to give individual dogs – just try to judge when your dog has had enough. Never walk puppies or young dogs to exhaustion; simply try to take the edge off their enthusiasm.

If your dog seems unable to tolerate moderate exercise without becoming tired out, or comes home lame for no obvious reason, consult the vet rather than simply assuming it is unfit. It may have a problem in its chest, muscles or bones (see also pp.78–9).

Toys

Play is a vital element in the development of a puppy. Since you won't always be on hand to amuse it, it needs to learn to play by itself. Providing proper toys prevents its desire to chew being directed towards you or your slippers. There are plenty of special pet toys on the market and older dogs enjoy them too. Puppies love the special rawhide chews which help give relief during teething.
Which toys are safe?
Toys that are safe for your pet vary according to the size of breed. All dogs love balls, but don't give them small ones. A tennis ball size is relatively safe; smaller balls could lodge at the back of a dog's throat and obstruct its airway. Football or softball types are the safest. Nylon bones are fine for most puppies and adult dogs of larger breeds, and squeaky toys give great pleasure – if you can bear the noise!

Toys are bound to suffer a certain amount of chewing and clawing, so use your common sense when buying them and keep these points in mind:
● Toys must be non-toxic.
● There must be no pieces which can be chewed off and swallowed.
● There should be no sharp edges.
● It should be impossible for the dog to swallow the whole toy.
● Beware of small balls or small, plastic childrens' toys.

The importance of games
Dogs love playing, especially with children.

Travelling with a dog

Most dogs need to travel at some stage in their life; many enjoy it.

Travelling by car
Some dogs take to cars well but some are soon car-sick and others become distressed immediately. Try to get your dog used to car travel from puppyhood.

Dogs are usually best confined behind a dog grille. Travelling boxes are only used routinely for small dogs or big dogs travelling by air or rail.

Travelling by air
Air travel is fairly cheap for dogs. Its speed minimizes the period of distress and your dog is never more than a few hours away from a vet. All dogs must travel in a container which complies with regulations laid down by airlines through the International Air Transport Association (I.A.T.A.).

Travelling abroad and rabies
When transporting a dog to another country, investigate the quarantine regulations in the countries you are travelling to and from. The U.K. is one of the world's few rabies-free countries and has strict quarantine laws. When you bring a dog to the U.K. from abroad, it will be quarantined for six months and given two anti-rabies innoculations.

TIPS FOR LONG JOURNEYS

- Before a long trip, give the dog a chance to urinate and defecate
- Give it a drink and something to eat before departure – about one third of its normal meal is enough. Some dogs can't eat anything before travelling but you'll discover this through trial and error
- Stop at reasonable intervals along the route – at least every 2–3 hours – to give the dog a chance to stretch, relieve itself and have a drink
- On very long trips, give the dog some more food after 4–5 hours. A little food in the stomach helps many dogs settle

A sturdy dog grille allows both you and your dog to travel comfortably, even over long distances.

Toilet training

Begin house-training as soon as you obtain a new puppy. As it will relieve itself frequently, there will probably be quite a few "accidents" before the puppy is trained. But never punish it if it relieves itself in the wrong place – you could cause a tiresome behavioural problem such as submissive urination.

Success depends on your predicting the call of nature. Common times are after activity, waking or eating. Some dogs circle and sniff the floor first.

If an adult dog arriving in your home is not well house-trained, be patient and start from the beginning.

House-training

If you are at home most of the time and access to the outside is easy, this is the simplest method.

Take the puppy out when it wakes, after every meal, when it has been active, if it hasn't urinated for some time or if it shows signs of wishing to do so. Let the puppy walk out with you rather than being carried, since it will then recognize the route and learn to go to the door when it needs to go out.

Until the puppy is able to go through the night without accidents, put newspaper by the door at night. You'll soon be able to discard it.

PAPER-TRAINING

If you live in a flat, or are out for much of the day, then paper-training is a good idea. It also makes a back-up to house-training.

The aim is to teach the puppy to relieve itself indoors on newspaper, which you can eventually place outside. When the frequency of urination and defecation is reduced to the level where you can be sure of being present when the puppy needs to go out, progress to full house-training. Some puppies dislike the feel of newspaper under their feet, particularly those that circle before relieving themselves. In this case it is probably best to go straight to house-training.

1 Confine the puppy to an easily cleaned room, and cover the floor with newspaper. When the puppy develops a preference for one area, remove the paper from the rest of the floor. You can then gradually move the paper, and eventually place it by the door.

2 On a fine day, place the paper outside. The next day, remove the paper altogether. Hopefully the puppy will then relieve itself outside. Praise it when it does this. Keep an eye out for the warning signs, including the puppy looking for its paper near the doorway.

Training: the first commands

There is no fixed age to begin training, but the best time to learn walking to heel is probably at about 12–14 weeks (when vaccination is under way). It usually takes about three months to train a young dog with no ingrained bad habits; older dogs take longer. Lead training is the first step and very few puppies actually enjoy it. However, getting it right is vital for

TEACHING YOUR DOG TO WALK TO HEEL

1 Be very calm and help your dog to get over its initial reaction by speaking reassuringly and holding the lead firmly. Shorten the lead and insist that the dog comes in to the required position, its right shoulder beside your left leg. Don't let the dog chew the lead – a bad habit which should be discouraged.

2 Having established mastery of the lead and your dog's movements, begin walking in a straight line. As you start off, say "HEEL" firmly. Continue speaking in a pleasant way to reassure your dog that all is well even though it may feel that something strange is happening! Check your dog if it pulls forward or hangs back.

3 At this stage, make any turns carefully. Initially, restrict yourself to making right turns – away from your dog. Turning to the left can panic it at first since it may worry about becoming entangled with your legs. Once your dog is used to walking on the lead, introduce the left turn.

the future. You and your dog will both enjoy going for walks far more if it is able to walk to heel willingly. Training sessions should be no longer than ten minutes for puppies and twenty for adult dogs, or the animal will lose interest. In fact, the first sessions should only last five minutes and can be repeated several times daily for the first few days, before you progress to ten minutes. Speak reassuringly, take your time, and give commands firmly.

Make sure no-one interferes with your training session. Puppies get confused if the whole family are involved, so decide on one person to be responsible for training. The rest of the family can learn the commands later.

WALKING: OUT AND ABOUT

After a few quiet sessions training your puppy to walk to heel, take it out on the streets and let it see other people. Everyone will want to pet the puppy. This encourages boisterous behaviour because it then expects everyone you meet to make a fuss of it. If possible, don't stop.

When you see other dogs, just keep walking. Obviously avoiding them makes the puppy think they're a threat, which can lead to aggression.

How soon you expose a young dog to noisy traffic and crowds depends on its temperament, but it is an important part of training. Don't begin too soon, or the dog will see it as a punishment.

Walking don'ts
- Don't stop to talk to people
- Don't allow sniffing of lamp posts
- Don't avoid other dogs
- Don't go among traffic and crowds too soon

TEACHING YOUR DOG TO SIT

When your dog is able to walk to heel properly and enthusiastically, continue the training process with the "SIT". When walking to heel, choose a quiet place to stop. Place your left hand on the dog's back, just above the pelvis, and apply gentle but firm pressure to make the dog sit. As you do this, say "SIT". Soon you can dispense with the lead and the hand.

Remember that dogs don't speak English. Saying "SIT" over and over again won't make your dog automatically understand. You must *show* it what you mean as well.

Hold your lead hand up

Bend your knees slightly

Training: the next steps

Once your dog has mastered "SIT" and will do it on command without your hand or the lead, it is time to introduce "STAY". This is an important landmark in your dog's training. By staying still while you go out of sight, the dog shows its total trust in you. Then, when you have taught it to stay, with the implication that you will return for it, it is useful to teach your dog the alternative command – "WAIT – COME".

TEACHING YOUR DOG TO STAY

1 Walk with your dog to heel, then make it sit. Holding the lead vertical and taut, command "STAY" and walk round the dog. Correct any attempt to move with a gentle but firm jerk of the lead. Repeat the command as you move round the dog. When it begins to understand, slacken the lead and widen your walking circle.

2 Now try the "SIT – STAY" command without the lead, again gradually extending your distance from your dog. To reinforce the command, stretch one arm away from your body, palm upwards, towards the dog. This psychologically lessens the gap between you. Gradually go further away until you are actually out of sight. When you return, praise the dog for its obedience, then continue walking.

TEACHING YOUR DOG TO WAIT AND COME

Don't be too anxious to try this without the lead as, initially, the command is easily broken. Your dog may push its luck and refuse to come, or sit just out of range. In this case, punishment is no use. Go back to lead training for a while. Remember never to scold your dog if it doesn't come on odd occasions – it should never be afraid to come to you. Always praise it when it does come – this is an important lesson.

For this exercise, you'll need a long lead – use the extending type if you have one, or extend your regular lead with 10–15 metres of nylon cord.

1 The procedure for learning "WAIT" is the same as for "STAY", so your dog will learn this quickly. Command the dog to sit and when it sits, command "WAIT", then turn and walk away.

2 Once you're a few metres away, turn and call the dog by name, stressing the additional command, "COME". You may need to give a little tug on the lead to show your dog what you mean.

TEACHING YOUR DOG TO LIE DOWN

This is usually comparatively simple to teach. The "DOWN" position is a natural extension of the "SIT" position. Use the lead in the same way as for "STAY".

Start with the "SIT" command. Now show the dog the "DOWN" position by moving its front legs at the same time as giving the "DOWN" command repeatedly, and gently reassuring the dog. Praise it if it maintains this position, but not if it gets up.

At first, it is important to show your dog the meaning of "DOWN"

Basic grooming

If you're the prospective owner of a long-haired breed such as Lhasa Apso, an Old English Sheepdog or an Afghan Hound, don't delude yourself over the amount of grooming time required. Up to an hour's work may be involved daily, and you should be prepared for this, or choose a breed which needs less grooming. If you intend to show your dog and it has one of the more "tricky" coats, the chances are it will need a certain amount of professional grooming as well as your routine care. Some breeds are better clipped professionally, but it certainly isn't essential for a pet dog.

The dog's coat

There are five basic types of dog coat – long, silky, non-shedding curly, smooth and wiry. To these we can add a sixth group of "extremes". Each type of coat has its own special grooming needs (see chart below right) but the principles of hair growth and the factors which produce a healthy coat are the same for all of them. The coat types requiring the most routine grooming are the curly coat, the wiry coat and any long-length coat.

The main aims of grooming are to remove dead hair and to clean the skin and the living hair. Every dog has several different types of hair on its body. Hairs grow in follicle complexes of several hairs per hole. In each follicle, there is a primary, or guard hair which belongs to the dog's outer coat, and several secondary hairs which constitute the undercoat. Other more specialized and sensitive hairs – the "tactile hairs" – are the eyelashes, the hair on the external ear, and the whiskers on the muzzle. For problems relating to the coat, see pp.80–1.

Moulting

Moulting – loss of hair and a change of coat – usually happens in Spring and Autumn, lasting four to six weeks. The new coat grows in three or four months. While your dog is moulting, groom it daily. A little dandruff is no problem, but with an excess, bath it.

Hair streams
The direction of hair growth follows lines called "hair streams", which run from the head, down the back, spreading down the body and legs to the feet. You can feel these if you stroke the dog.

COAT TYPE	GROOMING NEEDS
Long with undercoat	Bath Spring and Autumn. Brush and comb coat forwards, then back. Comb undercoat.
Silky	Brush and bath frequently. Trim or strip every three months.
Non-shedding curly	Clip and bath every six to eight weeks. Brush short areas every two days; comb longer parts before brushing.
Smooth	Comb and bristle brush or use a hound glove regularly.
Wiry	Comb regularly. Strip, pluck and bath every three to four months or clip every six to eight weeks.

BASIC GROOMING PROCEDURE

Here's a useful step-by-step reference plan for a "top-to-toe" grooming session for all types of dog.

Although you don't need to carry out all the steps at every session, it helps to know the right sequence in which to perform the various tasks for the best results. The needs of different coat types are described on p.24. For how to use the various tools, see pp.26–9.

1 Use a wide-toothed comb to break up the coat and remove mats.

2 Use a fine comb under the chin and tail and behind the ears.

3 Brush as required for the breed, following hair streams.

4 Strip or pluck the coat with a dresser or stripping knife.

5 Use scissors to tidy hair round eyes, genitals and anus.

6 Thin the coat with scissors or shears if required.

7 Bath or dry shampoo the dog (see p.28 for correct techniques).

8 Give the entire coat a final brush to help it to lie smoothly.

Grooming equipment

At the very least, every dog needs its own brush and comb for grooming. Brushes fall into the category of bristle types, hound gloves and carders. Brushes and combs are the main tools you need, but several others are available for different coat types – mostly cutting tools. Stripping combs, knives, scissors and shears can all be useful, whether your dog needs a trim, a thinning out, or just a routine tidy-up. Electric clippers are probably best restricted to professional use.

Keep your equipment in a dry box to prevent scissors and knives rusting. Each time you finish a grooming session, clean hair and grease off your tools before putting them away.

Fine comb

Bristle brush

Wide-toothed comb

Carder

Hound glove

USING A COMB

Combs are available in metal or plastic, although the plastic type often ends up broken and can be chewed by dogs. Whatever the comb is made of, the teeth should be rounded, both at the tips and in cross section, to avoid tearing the skin or hair. All dogs need a wide-toothed comb with teeth about 2 mm apart; finer-coated dogs and breeds prone to mats and tangles should have a finer comb too.

1 Insert the wide-toothed comb to its full depth into the coat and use it to break up any coarse mats or snags, particularly in the outer coat.

2 Use the finer comb to separate the undercoat and bring out any dead hair which is no longer firmly attached. Don't pull too hard, or you'll hurt the dog.

3 If you encounter any resistance in the coat, take the comb out, and work on the knot a little at a time, teasing it apart with the wide comb or your fingers.

USING A BRISTLE BRUSH

This is the tool used for the bulk of routine grooming. It is useful for "finishing off" after combing, particularly on the longer-coated breeds, and for giving a well-groomed dog a quick "once-over" after a run. The bristles should always be long enough to reach through the dog's coat to its skin. An inadequate brush may cause mats.

Short, dense-bristled brushes are fine for short-haired breeds. To brush a smooth-coated dog, follow the normal "lay" of the hair and the direction of the hair streams, beginning at the dog's head and working back towards the tail. If your dog has a long coat, you'll need a brush with longer, wider-spaced bristles set in a rubber base.

Professional groomers are wary of synthetic bristles, believing that they generate too much static electricity and cause hair breakage, so it is worth buying a genuine bristle brush if possible.

Brushing a long coat
On long-haired dogs and breeds whose hair is meant to stand out from their body, brush gently against the "lay" of the coat. Push the brush into the coat and twist it *slightly* against the natural growth, working in very short strokes. Never brush the whole coat in the wrong direction – you'll weaken or break hairs.

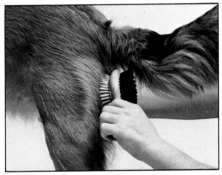

Brushing a medium coat
With medium-length coats (such as a Labrador's), pay particular attention to the hindquarters. The guard hairs in these coats are long enough to retain dead hair, and the dog's movements and its licking can make this move within the coat towards the dog's hindquarters where it accumulates in dense pads.

Using a carder
This is a kind of wire-bristled brush, consisting of a rectangular board with short, bent wire teeth mounted on it, and a handle. The function of the carder is to bring out dead undercoat on shorter-haired breeds. Use it in a similar way to the brush on long-haired dogs, working the teeth gently through to the skin and then twisting the carder out towards the surface.

Using a hound glove
Hound gloves are useful for short-haired dogs, particularly the hound types, to give a polish to the outer coat and to remove any dead undercoat. The glove has short bristles, wires or rubber bumps set into it, and you can slide your hand inside it, giving you a "bristled palm". A hound glove isn't really effective on coats longer than that of a Labrador.

Bathing and additional care

There's no simple answer to the question "How often should I bath my dog?" A dirty or smelly dog needs a bath, although a little dirt can often be brushed out when dry. Many dogs need more baths in summer, others need a regular monthly bath, but few need a bath more often than this. Always groom a dog before bathing it, or you could make matting much worse. Never use detergent or carbolic soap; many dogs' skins react badly to these. You can use a mild "human" soap, but a special dog shampoo or baby shampoo is best. The water should be comfortably warm. You can use your own bath (wash it well afterwards). A baby bath is ideal for smaller dogs.

Dry shampoo is good for a quick clean but doesn't deal with a really dirty dog properly. Dust the powder well into the dog's fur and brush it out. It removes excess oil, brightens the colour and enhances any white parts.

Using stripping tools

Stripping combs ("dressers") and stripping knives all provide a serrated metal cutting edge for removing dull, dead hair. The correct technique for use is to grasp a section of the dog's hair between the comb or knife and your thumb and pull the tool away with a twisting motion. Dead hair comes out, while live hair is trimmed.

Clipping a dog's nails

It is often a good idea to clip your pet's nails at the same time as other routine grooming. Use the guillotine type of clippers that cut, rather than the pliers type that crush. Crushing a nail can cause pain to the sensitive nail bed inside. The length of the nail bed varies in dogs, and if cut, it will hurt and bleed. Err on the side of caution and learn by any which you cause to bleed. If the dew claws have not been removed, check these too.

HOW TO BATH A DOG

1 Try and enlist the help of someone else to hold the dog steady while you shampoo it. Take off the collar and place the dog in the bath. Using a jug, shower attachment or slow-running hosepipe, wet the dog's back and work the water into the coat on back and sides.

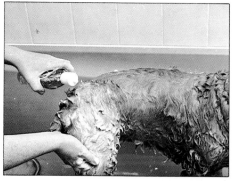

2 Apply some shampoo to the back and work it in, extending all the way to the rear of the dog and down the legs. Wash the head last, being careful not to get any shampoo in the dog's eyes. It is when its head gets wet that it is most likely to want to shake!

DEALING WITH MATS AND TANGLES

Small tangles can usually be teased apart with a wide-toothed comb. Once broken up, they should be thoroughly combed, first with the wide-toothed comb, then with a finer one.

Large mats which don't respond to this treatment can simply be removed by sliding a comb under the mat and cutting with scissors just above it. The result can be messy, and you may prefer to try dividing the mat with a knife or scissors, teasing it out in sections, then combing it. You can have this done professionally.

Removing a tangle from the coat
Lift the knot gently before you cut.

Special care for long-haired dogs

If you're using carders, hound gloves and short bristle brushes on your long-haired dog, you may not be grooming it properly at all. Although the outer coat may look smooth the hidden undercoat can build up into dense mats if tools don't reach it.

A dog that has been "surface-groomed" like this looks fine for a time but feels uncomfortable; eventually its outer coat becomes involved in the underlying mat. At this stage, the only answer is to shave the coat – a time-consuming job which upsets the dog. It may have to be done at the vet's surgery under anaesthetic and can be costly.

Shaving an Afghan is particularly tragic and is impossible to do neatly – the dog may take as long as 18 months to come back into coat. It may need steroid treatment for bruising caused by parting its matted coat from its skin. The moral of this is: never neglect the grooming of your long-haired dog. Make sure you're using the right tools and techniques.

3 Now rinse the dog thoroughly, starting with the head and working back. Squeeze out any excess water. In summer, a good run in the open air followed by a brush is enough to dry off most dogs, although long-haired dogs will need some towelling.

4 In winter, towel your dog and let it dry somewhere warm, otherwise it could catch a chill. You can use a hair-dryer, but be very careful introducing the dog to it – the noise and sensation may frighten it. Don't hold the dryer too close to the dog.

FEEDING

Your dog needs the right foods for growth, work and body maintenance. And a correctly balanced diet is all part of owning a happy, healthy dog with bright eyes and a well-conditioned coat. You'll soon be able to tell if you're not doing it right!

The principles of feeding a dog are the same as for all animals. There are a few nutritional differences between dogs, cats and humans, for instance, but these are to do with detailed requirements of specific nutrients. All dogs need certain nutritional components in the right proportions. Whether you're using pre-packed dog foods or giving your dog a home-cooked diet, feeding do's and don'ts should be carefully observed. It's important to adopt the right approach to amounts of food, energy requirements, drinking water, supplementation, feeding bowls, titbits and mealtimes. For advice on nutritional disorders, see p.61.

Providing a healthy diet

The aims of feeding your dog properly are important. They are to provide sufficient food for body maintenance plus enough for extras like growth, work, pregnancy and lactation (feeding a litter of puppies). Whether you feed your dog on pre-packed foods or a home-cooked diet, you must be sure your dog is getting enough of the nutritional components it needs.

The idea that "we are what we eat" applies to dogs as well as people. Dogs can be considered in terms of certain "raw materials" – the same nutritional components which make up its diet, plus water. These are □ Protein □ Fat □ Carbohydrate □ Vitamins □ Minerals □ Fibre. Each of these contributes in a different way to the health of the dog.

The value of protein
All animal tissue contains a relatively high level of protein, so your dog needs a continual supply to live and grow.

Unexpectedly for a carnivore, the dog's ability to digest protein is variable. Although most offal and fresh meat is 90 to 95 per cent digestible, dogs only digest 60 to 80 percent of vegetable protein. Too much vegetable protein can cause colic or diarrhoea.

The value of fat
Fats in the diet are present as fatty acids. Some of them are essential to the dog. A fatty acid deficiency causes an itchy skin or a harsh, dry coat with dandruff, often leading to ear infection. Dullness and nervousness are other possible effects.

Apart from being necessary for important metabolic processes, fat is an important energy source for dogs. Obtaining most of its energy from fats means a dog's protein intake can be reduced, lessening the demands on the liver and kidney. Fats are virtually 100 percent digestible for dogs and increase the palatability of their food.

The value of carbohydrates
Carbohydrates incorporate sugars, starch and cellulose. Dogs can derive quite high levels of energy from the carbohydrates in some foods. Very high levels are contained in boiled potatoes, rice and carrots, with dry dog food mixer and wholemeal bread a little lower on the list. All-meat canned food, fresh meat and fish have no carbohydrate-derived energy, but meat/cereal canned dog food and complete dry food contain 30 to 50 and 40 to 50 percent respectively.

Digestibility varies – the simplest sugars are the easiest for dogs to digest. They cannot digest lactose (sugar naturally present in milk) and too much milk causes diarrhoea, although they can cope quite well with sucrose (ordinary sugar).

The value of vitamins and minerals
Vitamins are essential for good health, and the vitamin level in prepared dog foods is carefully balanced. For dogs needing extra, there are very good proprietary supplements available.

Some minerals are needed in large amounts and others in trace amounts. Calcium and phosphorus are closely related and are two of the most important minerals in the dog's diet, needed for bone formation and development. It is important to supply enough but not too much; over-supplementation in larger breeds can cause bone deformities and diseases like rickets (see p.59).

The functions of fibre

High-fibre diets have become popular for humans and fibre is also helpful for dogs. A dog should be given about five percent of its total diet as fibre (dry weight). Fibre is valuable because it:
- Increases the rate of food passage through the gut (reduces problems of diarrhoea or wind)
- Aids digestion (even though food is passing through the system faster)
- Eases metabolic stress in liver disease (adsorbs toxic by-products of digestion)
- Acts as a bulking agent for obese dogs (same as slimming tablets for humans). Use as ten to 15 percent of the reducing diet (see p.37).
- Controls and eases absorption of glucose after a meal for diabetic dogs; use as ten to 15 percent of the diet.

How much food does my dog need?

You may feel tempted to promote your dog's growth by giving it large quantities of food. Seeking maximum growth, particularly in large and giant breeds, can cause serious growth abnormalities and may contribute towards their shorter lifespans.

It isn't a good idea to give your dog as much food as it wants to eat. The quantity which seems to produce the best results in terms of growth is about 80 percent of what it would eat if unchecked. More than this can cause obesity; less may curb growth.

The energy needs of a dog

The amount of food a dog eats is based on its energy needs. All dogs have different metabolic rates – the rate at which they turn food into energy by digesting protein, carbohydrate and fat. Like humans, dogs become fat if they take in more food-energy than they can "burn up" by exercise, so keep an eye open for obesity problems.

The energy is measured in kilocalories (kcals). For guidelines on daily feeding amounts for different dogs of various weights, based on their energy needs, see the table below. The values should be increased for the following:
- Growing puppies × 2–2.5
- Pregnancy (6–9 weeks) × 1.5
- Lactation × 3–4

The table on p.36 shows the breakdown of each type of pre-packed food in terms of protein, carbohydrate, fat and water. It also gives the energy content of each food in kilocalories per gram. Use the two tables together to calculate daily requirements of specific food types of your dog.

Where does the energy come from?
Most of the energy in dry dog foods comes from carbohydrates (50 percent), with the remaining 50 percent split between protein and fat. In semi-moist products, most of the energy comes from protein. Available energy in complete canned foods is well balanced between the three main elements, but in all-meat canned food, it is fat which provides 52 percent of the total available energy, protein 41 percent and carbohydrate only seven percent.

ENERGY REQUIREMENTS

Dog weight (kg)		Energy needed (kcals per day)
small breeds	2	230
	5	450
	10	750
medium breeds	15	1010
	20	1250
	25	1470
large breeds	30	1675
	35	1875
	40	2070

Feedtime techniques

Most adult dogs over 12 months have one feed per day, usually given in the evening. Some small breeds will only eat a small amount at one "sitting" and need two meals daily. Overfeeding a dog may result in vomiting or diarrhoea. Dogs will obligingly fit in with the household routine and are often happy to be fed at around the same time as the rest of the family. This helps to prevent them from scrounging for food while you're eating your own meal.

Unfortunately, after an evening feed, some dogs can't get through the night without needing to relieve themselves – an apparent breakdown in your careful house-training. The answer to this problem is usually to change the feeding regime – moving feedtime to earlier in the day, or giving half the food early and half in the evening. For guidelines on feeding puppies and young dogs, seek your vet's advice.

Where to feed your dog

A dog likes to have a regular feeding place. This enforces its routine and encourages it not to take too long over its meal.

Where to feed your dog is a matter of personal preference. Most dogs are tidy eaters, but it is sensible to choose a place which is easy to clean – such as a kitchen or conservatory floor or an outside covered area. You can place food and water bowls on a wipe-down plastic mat. Some dogs like to pull pieces of meat from their bowl and sit on the floor chewing them like a lion with its kill. Put down newspaper for these dogs otherwise you'll have to clean the floor after every meal. Don't leave uneaten meals on the floor too long – they'll be dry and tasteless.

FEEDING TWO OR MORE DOGS

If you have more than one dog, each should have its own bowl and be fed a little way away from the others. Discourage dogs from sharing each other's bowls; the practice can lead to the following problems:
- One dog may become overweight through eating the "lion's share"
- Diffident dogs get pushed out
- Individual dogs may need diet supplements
- Fights can occur, even if dogs are used to communal feeding
- It is difficult to detect a dog off its food through illness, since the other dog often eats what's left

Need for water

Water is crucial to all animals. On a weight for weight basis, most dogs' bodies consist of about two thirds water. Fatter dogs may drop to 50 percent water, leaner ones can be as much as 75 percent water. All dogs lose water from their body through: sweating, panting, via the gut, via the lungs and via the kidneys. This must be replaced, and so you should make sure that fresh water is always available for your dog.

How much water is needed?

To maintain the correct balance, a healthy dog should take in about 40 ml per kg of body weight per day. This can come from all sources including the moisture contained in food.

Weight of dog	Water needed per day
10 kg	400 ml
20 kg	800 ml
30 kg	1200 ml
40 kg	1600 ml

Your dog will want to drink more water in hot weather when water loss through panting and the lungs is increased. More is also needed in dogs with diarrhoea or kidney disease. The tabled quantities are merely guidelines and you should know the amount of water your dog normally drinks.

There are several diseases of which thirst is a common symptom. If you notice excessive thirst, contact your vet as soon as convenient.

Eating between meals

Don't accustom your dog to tit-bits between meals; this only encourages begging and makes the dog a nuisance with visitors. Once the principle of "no scrounging" is established, you should have no problems. It's often more difficult training the family to accept this than your dog! Non-fatty scraps from the family meal can be placed in your dog's bowl for its next meal.

Tit-bits are best used as a reward for good behaviour or as a training aid.

Remember that tit-bits are still food and if used in excess can cause obesity, so make the gift a token only.

Suitable tit-bits are:
● Semi-moist dog food – only suitable given in very small amounts
● Special crunchy treats for dogs
● Chocolate drops – special dog chocolates – use in moderation
● Raisins – use in moderation
● Broken biscuit – very suitable
Warning Vitamin/mineral supplements are most unsuitable – an overdose can easily occur.

Bones
An occasional bone provides hours of pleasure and can help clean the teeth and exercise the jaw. The only safe bones are "knuckle" bones, which don't splinter.

TYPES OF FEEDING BOWL

Choosing a feeding bowl is a matter of personal preference and price. Plastic bowls are the cheapest, but are often scratched and chewed, making them difficult to clean properly. Stainless steel bowls are excellent for cleaning but can be knocked over as they're generally light. The familiar glazed earthenware bowl is both stable and easy to clean, although in time it can become chipped and will obviously break if dropped.

Breeds with long, floppy ears like spaniels, Bassets and setters sometimes trail their ears in their food bowls – a practice that can cause dermatitis on the ear flaps. Special deep, narrow feeding bowls are available to exclude the ears from the feed and avoid this problem.

Dogs which are inclined to choke while feeding because of soft-palate problems combined with their eagerness to eat fast may be more comfortable with their food bowl raised a few inches off the ground. This keeps the head up and encourages the food to go in the right direction.

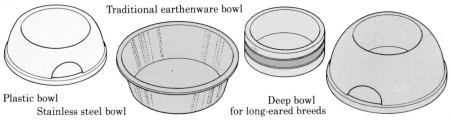

Traditional earthenware bowl

Plastic bowl
Stainless steel bowl

Deep bowl
for long-eared breeds

Food types

There are three main types of prepared dog food: dry, semi-moist and canned. Pre-packed foods are well balanced and generally of very high quality.

Dry foods

Despite their name, these contain about ten percent water. Although all brands have a similar nutritional analysis, they contain a variety of raw materials, so some may be more palatable or digestible than others.

Advantages include low cost – a bonus if you have a large dog. Dry food can be stored in quantities to last several weeks; kept for too long, however, it may go off and lose its vitamin content. Dry foods are high in bulk and can help dogs which suffer from dietary upsets. One word of warning – they're initially easy to overfeed, causing obesity.

Semi-moist foods

Sometimes called "soft-moist", these foods contain about 25 percent water. Presented as simulated mince or chunks of meat, they're often more acceptable to owners than dry diets because they do look more like meat. Semi-moist foods come packed in average servings and store well without refrigeration. They can be rather expensive but provide a good alternative for dogs used to fresh meat if this becomes difficult to obtain. Some rather fussy small dogs love them. They have a high sugar level, and so are unsuitable for diabetic dogs.

Canned foods

To most people, this is probably the most familiar form of dog food, but many don't realize that there are two types which must be fed differently.
Complete canned food
These have a cereal component which makes them a complete diet.
All-meat diet
These need added biscuits to make them a balanced food. Feeding an all-meat diet without adding biscuit is expensive since you need more food to satisfy the dog. And despite the extra cost, it isn't nutritionally balanced.
Biscuits
Dogs which won't eat biscuit with their meal will often eat separate dog biscuits. It is quite in order to feed your dog an all-meat food and supplement this during the day with dog biscuits given as tit-bits.

ANALYSIS OF PRE-PACKED DOG FOODS

Type of food	Percentage in food of:				Total energy (kcals per gram)
	Protein	Carbohydrate	Fat	Water	
Dry (complete)	22	51	7	15	3.4
Semi-moist	19	38	10	26	3.0
Canned (complete)	8.2	12	4.8	72.5	1.0
Canned (all-meat)	9.3	1.5	4.7	81.9	1.3
Biscuit	10	69.9	6.1	8.4	average 3.5

Individual products may vary from these values but manufacturers will normally supply analyses on request.

Vitamin and mineral supplements

Most pre-packed dog foods need no extra supplementation except under particular circumstances such as convalescence, pregnancy, lactation and growth. However, fresh diets do need extra vitamins and minerals. This simple supplement can be added to lights, melts, heart, liver, egg, table scraps, bread and vegetables, and provides the required level for each kilogram of fresh food:

- 2–3 teaspoons bonemeal
- 2000–3000 I.U. Vitamin A
- 200–300 I.U. Vitamin D

Proprietary supplements
There are so many of these that it is safest to choose a well-known brand. Never exceed the manufacturer's dose.

Eggs
These are a good source of easily digestible protein. Don't feed raw egg white; it impairs B vitamin absorption.

Milk
A good protein and calcium source, although it may cause diarrhoea in some adult dogs lacking the enzyme to digest lactose.

Vegetable oil
Some vegetable oils are rich in linoleic acid (an essential fatty acid). When dogs are deficient in this, their coats become dull and poor-looking. Most pre-packed foods provide more than the required one percent, but a little extra does no harm.

Cod liver oil
A good vitamin source which should only be used in tiny amounts.

Yeast
Yeast preparations are rich in the B vitamins and some minerals. They're useful for older dogs or those with weak livers and are also safe used in excess.

Herbal preparations
Many are available, among them seaweed tablets, given for iodine.

Providing a home-cooked diet

It is perfectly possible to prepare a well-balanced diet for your dog at home. Using the basic meat and rice recipe below, suitable diets can be planned for a variety of circumstances.

Don't buy mince for adult dogs – it can contain too much fat. Medium-fat cuts or chunks of meat are best – you can mince these yourself.

Other foods
Nutritional balance is essential for your dog, but variety is not, so don't chop and change too much. Dogs benefit from a certain amount of vegetable matter in their diet, but are basically carnivores, so even if you yourself are vegetarian, you should not impose a vegetarian diet on your dog.

Non-fatty scraps from your own meals provide some acceptable variety, particularly leftover meat, stews and vegetables. Never give small bones.

BASIC HOME-COOKED DIET

(Quantity per 10kg dog weight)
$\frac{2}{3}$ teacup uncooked rice
$\frac{1}{3}$ teacup meat
6 teaspoons raw liver
1 teaspoon bonemeal
1 teaspoon corn oil
$\frac{1}{2}$ teaspoon iodised salt

Method
Mince the meat and cook in a little water. Boil the rice in water and mix it with the cooked meat. When this is cool, add remaining ingredients and feed to your dog warm or cold.

- **Meaty** For normal maintenance of small dogs and for large dogs needing extra for growth and work, halve the amount of rice and double the meat.
- **Reducing** For obese dogs, halve the amount of rice, use lean meat and add $\frac{2}{3}$ teacup wheat bran.
- **Geriatric** For older dogs, halve the amount of rice, use $\frac{1}{2}$ teacup meat and add $\frac{1}{2}$ teacup wheat bran.

3

HEALTH CARE

Every dog owner wants a healthy pet, but problems –
major or minor – are bound to arise from time to time.
It is important to understand the types of disorder
that can afflict your dog and how to observe the signs
of illness so that you can give an accurate description
to your vet. Basic signs of illness are dealt with in the
Diagnosis charts on pp.43–8. Use these to gain an
idea of what is wrong, how serious it is and what
action to take. Your dog relies on you for its health
and well-being. Make sure it has the appropriate
vaccinations to protect it against infectious diseases.
If you're in any doubt about its condition, contact the
vet. Once the vet has diagnosed the ailment and
treated your dog, it may need nursing at home.
Elderly dogs are prone to particular problems and
careful attention to these can make their remaining
years more comfortable. The techniques of first aid for
dogs are covered on pp.88–93.

How to use this chapter

The chapter begins with information that helps you to decide whether your dog is ill, including instructions on taking the temperature and pulse, and signs of ill-health. This is followed by the *Ailments* section, divided into areas of the body and systems within it. A section on care and nursing covers taking a sick dog to the vet, caring for an ill or elderly dog, and keeping your dog healthy. Lastly, a vital section deals with first aid.

Is my dog ill?
Dogs can't describe how they're feeling or what their symptoms are. As a dog owner, you're restricted to the clues that you can actually see – the *signs* of illness. So in this chapter, emphasis is placed on the "signs" of various problems and diseases, rather than their "symptoms".

Is my dog healthy?
There are a number of points on your dog that you should check regularly. A healthy dog has an upright stance and posture – it is alert, looking around and interested in its environment and in what is happening around it. The dog holds its head high and its ears follow sounds – you can sometimes see the ear flaps twitching. A healthy dog's nose is usually moist and there should be no discharges from its eyes or nose. The skin should look pink and healthy; the shine and depth of colour in the coat should be such that it just asks to be stroked. A healthy dog moves easily with no effort or lameness, and isn't overweight – there should be a little fat over the ribs so they don't "glare", but they should still be felt without difficulty.

AILMENTS SECTION

"See also" boxes These reference boxes lead you to relevant information in other sections of the book.

Quick-reference boxes These help you to make decisions when you spot signs of illness.

Urgency advice Crosses indicate how quickly you should contact a vet.

Special breed problems boxes If particular breeds are susceptible to certain problems, these are listed so you can watch out for them.

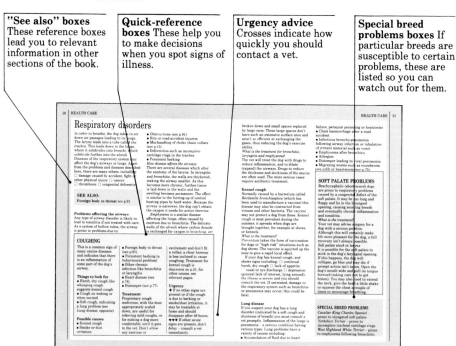

SIGNS OF ILLNESS

The first signs of ill-health you'll notice in your dog usually involve behaviour: it becomes duller, more introverted and less active. Also, its appetite is often affected and may decrease or increase.

Warning – acute signs: If your dog displays any of the following signs, consult a vet immediately: □ collapse □ vomiting repeatedly for more than 24 hours □ diarrhoea for longer than 24 hours □ troubled breathing □ bleeding from an orifice □ obvious pain.

The major signs of illness
□ Looking off-colour □ Vomiting □ Diarrhoea □ Troubled breathing □ Bleeding □ Scratching (see pp.231–6).

Other common signs of illness
On close examination, you may be able to detect other signs. If in doubt, watch out for the following:
Respiratory signs □ Coughing (see p.50)
Ear signs □ Painful ears (see p.65) □ Swollen ear flap (see p.64) □ Discharge (see p.65) □ Poor hearing (see p.65)
Eye signs □ Discharge (see p.67) □ Swollen eye (see p.67)
Body signs □ Limping (see p.78)
Skin signs □ Scratching (see p. 81) □ Reddened skin (see p.81) □ Hair loss (see p.81)
Bowel/urinary signs □ Constipation (see p.60) □ Incontinence (see p.71).

DIAGNOSIS CHARTS

Back-up information
Following the quick-reference boxes, you'll find more detailed information on specific problems.

Prevention boxes
Where relevant, preventative measures are given.

Answer the questions and follow the arrows to an endpoint that suggests a likely veterinary diagnosis.

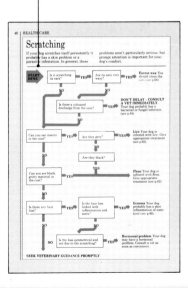

TAKING YOUR DOG'S TEMPERATURE

Don't rely on a dog's nose as a guide to its temperature or state of health. If you're unsure whether your dog is ill, taking its temperature is a useful guide as to whether or not you should contact the vet. The normal temperature is 38–9°C. Unless the dog is in a state of nervous excitement, which may push the temperature up very slightly, anything above this is abnormal and grounds for contacting your vet. Use a stubby-bulb thermometer (which doesn't break so easily as the more slender type).

1 Shake down the mercury in the thermometer to around 36°C.
2 Ask a helper to restrain the dog.
3 Lubricate the thermometer with a little petroleum jelly, or olive oil.
4 With one hand, raise the dog's tail slightly and move it to one side. Insert the thermometer about 2.5 cm into the rectum and hold it still, angled so that the bulb is against the rectal wall.
5 Wait 30 seconds, remove the thermometer and read it.
6 Shake it down, clean and disinfect it before replacing it in its case.

Inserting the thermometer
It is important to angle the thermometer correctly or you may damage the dog's rectum.

TAKING YOUR DOG'S PULSE

Measuring a dog's pulse gives you a direct count of the heart rate. The technique involves placing the ball of one or two fingers over an artery. The best place is the femoral artery on the inside of the thigh. In the centre of the upper thigh is a depression where the pulse can be felt as the femoral artery traverses the femur. However, with some dogs it is easier to feel the pulse over the heart area – low on the left-hand side of the chest (just behind the point of the elbow of a standing dog).

Use a watch with a second hand and count the number of beats in 30 seconds or one minute. Don't count for less time – multiplying to get the rate per minute may produce errors.

The pulse rate of small dogs is 90–120 beats per minute; large dogs have a slower rate of 65–90 beats.

Respiratory rate
When relaxed, your dog's normal rate of breathing should be around 10–30 breaths per minute (higher in small dogs than large dogs). Always be aware of your dog's breathing – it should be easy and smooth.

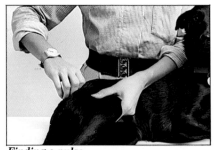

Finding a pulse
Try practising this when your dog is healthy, so that you know where to locate its pulse.

Looking off-colour

Your dog may show all the physical signs of health (see p.40) and yet not be itself. It may be off its food or show one or more of the signs below. If you're in any doubt about its health, telephone your vet or visit the surgery.

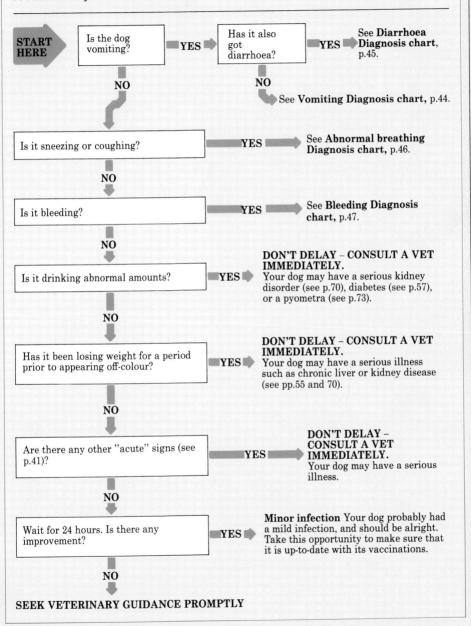

START HERE

Is the dog vomiting? — **YES** → Has it also got diarrhoea? — **YES** → See **Diarrhoea Diagnosis chart**, p.45.

NO (vomiting) ↓

NO (diarrhoea) → See **Vomiting Diagnosis chart**, p.44.

Is it sneezing or coughing? — **YES** → See **Abnormal breathing Diagnosis chart**, p.46.

NO ↓

Is it bleeding? — **YES** → See **Bleeding Diagnosis chart**, p.47.

NO ↓

Is it drinking abnormal amounts? — **YES** → **DON'T DELAY – CONSULT A VET IMMEDIATELY.** Your dog may have a serious kidney disorder (see p.70), diabetes (see p.57), or a pyometra (see p.73).

NO ↓

Has it been losing weight for a period prior to appearing off-colour? — **YES** → **DON'T DELAY – CONSULT A VET IMMEDIATELY.** Your dog may have a serious illness such as chronic liver or kidney disease (see pp.55 and 70).

NO ↓

Are there any other "acute" signs (see p.41)? — **YES** → **DON'T DELAY – CONSULT A VET IMMEDIATELY.** Your dog may have a serious illness.

NO ↓

Wait for 24 hours. Is there any improvement? — **YES** → **Minor infection** Your dog probably had a mild infection, and should be alright. Take this opportunity to make sure that it is up-to-date with its vaccinations.

NO ↓

SEEK VETERINARY GUIDANCE PROMPTLY

Vomiting

There are many causes of vomiting in dogs, ranging from the mild to the very serious. If you're in *any* doubt about your dog's health you should telephone your vet or visit the veterinary surgery immediately.

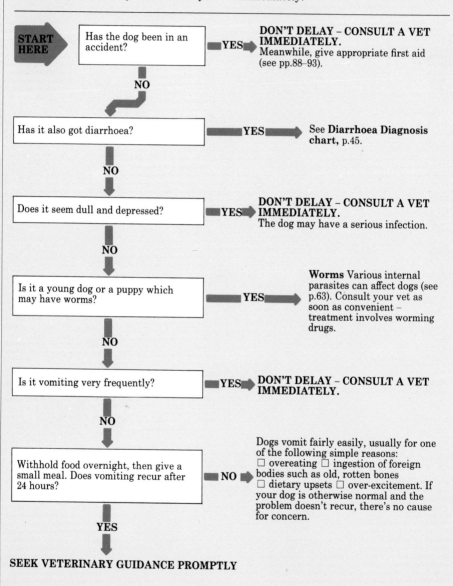

START HERE → Has the dog been in an accident? — **YES** → **DON'T DELAY – CONSULT A VET IMMEDIATELY.** Meanwhile, give appropriate first aid (see pp.88–93).

↓ **NO**

Has it also got diarrhoea? — **YES** → See **Diarrhoea Diagnosis chart**, p.45.

↓ **NO**

Does it seem dull and depressed? — **YES** → **DON'T DELAY – CONSULT A VET IMMEDIATELY.** The dog may have a serious infection.

↓ **NO**

Is it a young dog or a puppy which may have worms? — **YES** → **Worms** Various internal parasites can affect dogs (see p.63). Consult your vet as soon as convenient – treatment involves worming drugs.

↓ **NO**

Is it vomiting very frequently? — **YES** → **DON'T DELAY – CONSULT A VET IMMEDIATELY.**

↓ **NO**

Withhold food overnight, then give a small meal. Does vomiting recur after 24 hours? — **NO** → Dogs vomit fairly easily, usually for one of the following simple reasons: ☐ overeating ☐ ingestion of foreign bodies such as old, rotten bones ☐ dietary upsets ☐ over-excitement. If your dog is otherwise normal and the problem doesn't recur, there's no cause for concern.

↓ **YES**

SEEK VETERINARY GUIDANCE PROMPTLY

Diarrhoea

If your dog passes frequent liquid or semi-liquid motions it may be unwell. The cause is probably a minor infection but there's a possibility that it has something more serious. If you're in any doubt about your dog's health, you should telephone the vet or visit your veterinary surgery immediately.

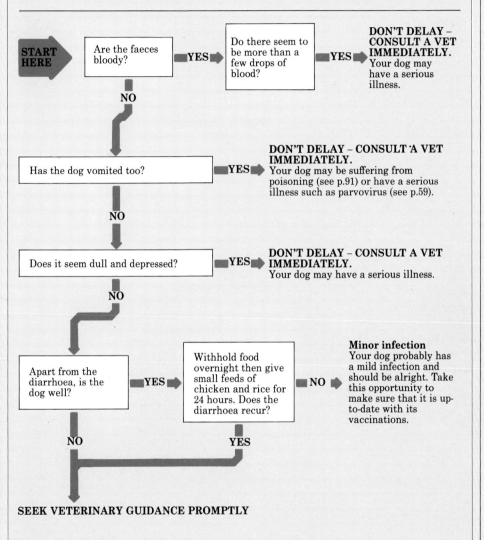

START HERE

Are the faeces bloody? → **YES** → Do there seem to be more than a few drops of blood? → **YES** → **DON'T DELAY – CONSULT A VET IMMEDIATELY.** Your dog may have a serious illness.

NO

Has the dog vomited too? → **YES** → **DON'T DELAY – CONSULT A VET IMMEDIATELY.** Your dog may be suffering from poisoning (see p.91) or have a serious illness such as parvovirus (see p.59).

NO

Does it seem dull and depressed? → **YES** → **DON'T DELAY – CONSULT A VET IMMEDIATELY.** Your dog may have a serious illness.

NO

Apart from the diarrhoea, is the dog well? → **YES** → Withhold food overnight then give small feeds of chicken and rice for 24 hours. Does the diarrhoea recur? → **NO** → **Minor infection** Your dog probably has a mild infection and should be alright. Take this opportunity to make sure that it is up-to-date with its vaccinations.

NO   **YES**

SEEK VETERINARY GUIDANCE PROMPTLY

Abnormal breathing

A healthy dog's breathing is quiet and even, and consists of 10–30 breaths per minute. If your dog's breathing doesn't seem normal it may have a health problem or merely be resting or affected by hot weather or exertion.

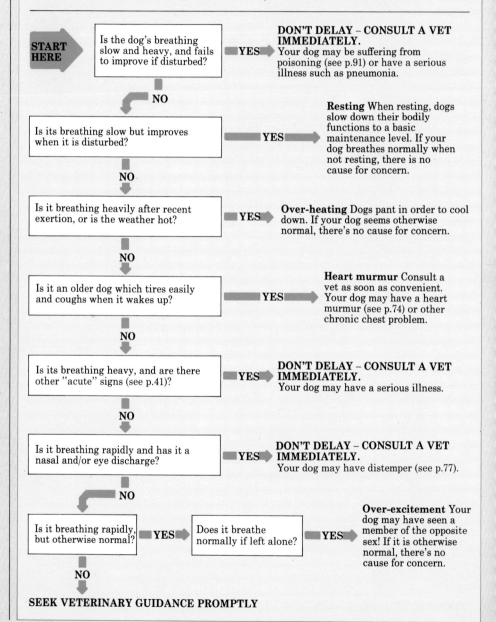

START HERE

Is the dog's breathing slow and heavy, and fails to improve if disturbed?

YES → **DON'T DELAY – CONSULT A VET IMMEDIATELY.** Your dog may be suffering from poisoning (see p.91) or have a serious illness such as pneumonia.

NO

Is its breathing slow but improves when it is disturbed?

YES → **Resting** When resting, dogs slow down their bodily functions to a basic maintenance level. If your dog breathes normally when not resting, there is no cause for concern.

NO

Is it breathing heavily after recent exertion, or is the weather hot?

YES → **Over-heating** Dogs pant in order to cool down. If your dog seems otherwise normal, there's no cause for concern.

NO

Is it an older dog which tires easily and coughs when it wakes up?

YES → **Heart murmur** Consult a vet as soon as convenient. Your dog may have a heart murmur (see p.74) or other chronic chest problem.

NO

Is its breathing heavy, and are there other "acute" signs (see p.41)?

YES → **DON'T DELAY – CONSULT A VET IMMEDIATELY.** Your dog may have a serious illness.

NO

Is it breathing rapidly and has it a nasal and/or eye discharge?

YES → **DON'T DELAY – CONSULT A VET IMMEDIATELY.** Your dog may have distemper (see p.77).

NO

Is it breathing rapidly, but otherwise normal? — **YES** → Does it breathe normally if left alone? — **YES** → **Over-excitement** Your dog may have seen a member of the opposite sex! If it is otherwise normal, there's no cause for concern.

NO

SEEK VETERINARY GUIDANCE PROMPTLY

Bleeding

If your dog is bleeding you must investigate the source and take immediate action as it may need urgent veterinary attention. Advice on applying bandages is given in the section dealing with first aid (see pp.88–93).

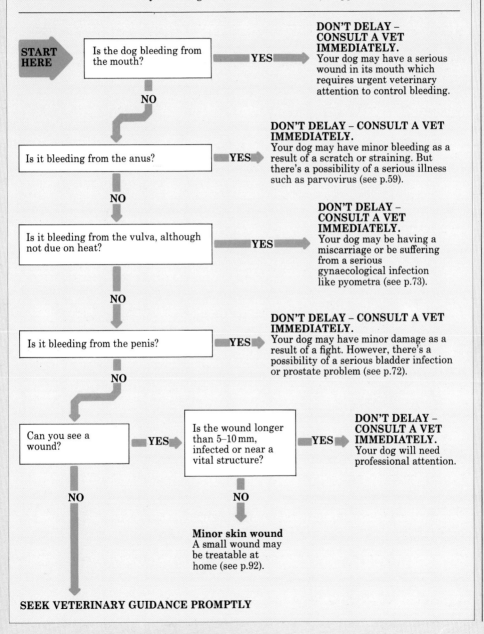

START HERE

Is the dog bleeding from the mouth? — **YES** — **DON'T DELAY – CONSULT A VET IMMEDIATELY.** Your dog may have a serious wound in its mouth which requires urgent veterinary attention to control bleeding.

NO

Is it bleeding from the anus? — **YES** — **DON'T DELAY – CONSULT A VET IMMEDIATELY.** Your dog may have minor bleeding as a result of a scratch or straining. But there's a possibility of a serious illness such as parvovirus (see p.59).

NO

Is it bleeding from the vulva, although not due on heat? — **YES** — **DON'T DELAY – CONSULT A VET IMMEDIATELY.** Your dog may be having a miscarriage or be suffering from a serious gynaecological infection like pyometra (see p.73).

NO

Is it bleeding from the penis? — **YES** — **DON'T DELAY – CONSULT A VET IMMEDIATELY.** Your dog may have minor damage as a result of a fight. However, there's a possibility of a serious bladder infection or prostate problem (see p.72).

NO

Can you see a wound? — **YES** — Is the wound longer than 5–10 mm, infected or near a vital structure? — **YES** — **DON'T DELAY – CONSULT A VET IMMEDIATELY.** Your dog will need professional attention.

NO   **NO**

Minor skin wound A small wound may be treatable at home (see p.92).

SEEK VETERINARY GUIDANCE PROMPTLY

Scratching

If your dog scratches itself persistently it probably has a skin problem or a parasitic infestation. In general, these problems aren't particularly serious, but prompt attention is important for your dog's comfort.

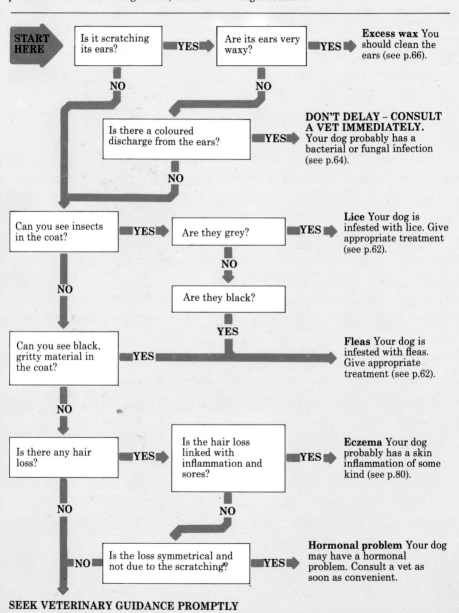

START HERE

Is it scratching its ears? → **YES** → Are its ears very waxy? → **YES** → **Excess wax** You should clean the ears (see p.66).

NO ↓   **NO** ↓

Is there a coloured discharge from the ears? → **YES** → **DON'T DELAY – CONSULT A VET IMMEDIATELY.** Your dog probably has a bacterial or fungal infection (see p.64).

NO ↓

Can you see insects in the coat? → **YES** → Are they grey? → **YES** → **Lice** Your dog is infested with lice. Give appropriate treatment (see p.62).

NO ↓   **NO** ↓

Are they black?

YES ↓

Can you see black, gritty material in the coat? → **YES** → **Fleas** Your dog is infested with fleas. Give appropriate treatment (see p.62).

NO ↓

Is there any hair loss? → **YES** → Is the hair loss linked with inflammation and sores? → **YES** → **Eczema** Your dog probably has a skin inflammation of some kind (see p.80).

NO ↓   **NO** ↓

Is the loss symmetrical and not due to the scratching? → **YES** → **Hormonal problem** Your dog may have a hormonal problem. Consult a vet as soon as convenient.

NO ↓

SEEK VETERINARY GUIDANCE PROMPTLY

AILMENTS

This section is divided into different areas and systems of the body. Where practical, quick-reference boxes give basic guidance to help you make decisions when you spot signs of illness in your dog. Crosses are used to denote the likely degree of urgency with which you should seek expert attention (this ranges from one cross for "may be treatable at home" to three crosses for "don't delay – consult a vet immediately"). Following the quick-reference boxes, detailed descriptions of common problems, diseases and treatments are given. Where applicable, preventative measures such as vaccinations and special diets are also included.

This guide isn't meant to be a substitute for professional veterinary care. Diagnosis depends on the particular circumstances of the individual dog and can only be made by a qualified veterinary surgeon. The aim of this chapter is to inform you of the degree of urgency and help you understand what is wrong with your dog once a diagnosis has been made. The information included represents an understanding of veterinary knowledge at the date of publication.

The vet's examination
Whenever you take your dog to the surgery, the vet will give it a thorough examination to check for signs of ill health or injury.

MAJOR INFECTIOUS DISEASES

There are four major infectious diseases of dogs, each discussed in this chapter under the system they primarily affect. They are:
Canine distemper, sometimes called "hardpad" which may ultimately affect the nervous system (see p.77)
Infectious canine hepatitis, sometimes called "Rubarth's disease" which affects the liver (see p.56)
Parvovirus which affects the intestines and bowel (see p.59)
Leptospirosis which affects the liver or kidney (see pp.56 and 71).

Apart from leptospirosis, these serious diseases are caused by viruses and so have no specific treatment as there might be for a bacterial disease. If your dog should contract any of these diseases, its body must fight the illness itself while you and your vet help with symptomatic treatment. The aim of vaccination is to *prevent* the dog catching the disease at all. In the rare cases where a dog can't resist the disease completely, prior vaccination usually reduces its severity.

All puppies should be vaccinated against the four major infectious diseases, usually beginning at eight to ten weeks. In addition, your dog should be protected by annual vaccination boosters. Keep in touch with your vet; be guided by him or her.

Respiratory disorders

In order to breathe, the dog takes in air down air passages leading to its lungs. The *larynx* leads into a tube called the *trachea*. This leads down to the lungs, where it subdivides into *bronchi*, which subdivide further into the *alveoli*. Diseases of the respiratory system may affect the dog's airways or lungs. Apart from the problems and diseases described here, there are many others, including: ☐ damage caused by accident, fight or other physical injury ☐ cancer ☐ thrombosis ☐ congenital deformity.

SEE ALSO:
Foreign body in throat see p.91.

Problems affecting the airways
Any type of airway disorder is likely to lead to tonsilitis if not treated with care. As a system of hollow tubes, the airway is prone to problems due to:

● Obstructions (see p.91)
● Bite or road-accident injuries
● Mis-handling of choke chain collars (see p.15)
● Deformities such as incomplete cartilage rings in the trachea
● Persistent barking

How disease affects the airways
There are several diseases which alter the anatomy of the larynx. In *laryngitis* and *bronchitis*, the walls are thickened, making the airway smaller. As this becomes more chronic, further tissue is laid down in the walls and the swelling becomes permanent. The effect is similar to the furring-up of central heating pipes by hard water. Because the airway is narrower, the dog can't obtain the oxygen it needs for active exercise.

Emphysema is a similar disease affecting the lungs, often caused by exertion due to bronchitis. The delicate walls of the alveoli where carbon dioxide is exchanged for oxygen in breathing, are

---

COUGHING

This is a common sign of many canine diseases and indicates that there is an inflammation of some part of the dog's airway.

Things to look for
● Harsh, dry cough like whooping cough suggests kennel cough
● Cough on waking or when excited
● Soft cough, indicating a lung problem (see *Lung disease*, opposite)

Possible causes
● Kennel cough
● Smoke or dust irritation

● Foreign body in throat (see p.91)
● Persistent barking (a behavioural problem)
● Other chronic infection like bronchitis or laryngitis
● Heart disease (see p.74)
● Distemper (see p.77)

Treatment
Proprietary cough medicines, with the dose appropriately scaled down, are useful for relieving mild coughs, or for making a dog more comfortable until it gets to the vet. Don't allow any exercise or

excitement and don't fit a collar; a chest harness is less inclined to cause coughing. Treatment for kennel cough is described on p.51; for other causes, see relevant pages.

Urgency
✚ If no other signs are present or if the cough is due to barking or smoke/dust irritation, it may be treatable at home and should disappear after 48 hours.
✚✚✚ If other acute signs are present, don't delay – consult a vet immediately.

broken down and small spaces replaced by large ones. These large spaces don't have such an extensive surface area and aren't so efficient at exchanging the gases, thus reducing the dog's exercise ability.

What is the treatment for bronchitis, laryngitis and emphysema?
The vet will treat the dog with drugs to reduce inflammation, and to dilate (expand) the airways. Drugs to reduce the thickness and stickiness of the mucus are often used. The more serious cases require antibiotic treatment.

Kennel cough
Normally caused by a bacterium called *Bordatella bronchiseptica* (which has been used to manufacture a vaccine) this disease may also be contracted from viruses and other bacteria. The vaccine may not protect a dog from these. Kennel cough is most prevalent during the summer; it spreads when dogs are brought together, for example at shows or kennels.

What is the treatment?
Prevention takes the form of vaccination for dogs in "high risk" situations such as dog shows. The vaccine is squirted up the nose to give a rapid local effect.

If your dog *has* kennel cough, and shows signs including: □ continual harsh, dry cough □ lack of appetite □ nasal or eye discharge □ depression (general lack of interest, lying around), the illness is severe and you should consult the vet. If untreated, damage to the respiratory system such as bronchitis or pneumonia may occur; this could be fatal.

Lung disease
If you suspect your dog has a lung disorder (indicated by a soft cough and shortness of breath) you must consult a vet promptly. Inflammation of the lungs is pneumonia – a serious condition having various types. Lung problems have a variety of causes including:
● Accumulation of fluid due to heart failure, paraquat poisoning or heatstroke
● Chest haemorrhage after a road accident
● Infectious broncho-pneumonia following airway infection or inhalation of irritant material such as vomit
● Emphysema after bronchitis
● Allergies
● Distemper leading to viral pneumonia
● Migrating worms such as roundworm (see p.63) or heartworm (see p.75).

SOFT PALATE PROBLEMS
Brachycephalic (short-nosed) dogs are prone to respiratory problems caused by a congenital defect of the soft palate. It may be too long and floppy and lie in the laryngeal opening, causing snorting breath and eventually chronic inflammation and tonsilitis.

What is the treatment?
Your vet may advise surgery for a dog with a serious problem. Although this will certainly make life more pleasant for the dog, a full recovery isn't always possible.

Soft palate stuck in larynx
It is possible for the soft palate to stick in the dog's laryngeal opening. If this happens, the dog will collapse, go blue and may die if prompt action isn't taken. Open the dog's mouth wide and pull its tongue forward (taking care not to get bitten). You may also need to extend the neck, give the head a little shake or squeeze the chest a couple of times to encourage breathing.

SPECIAL BREED PROBLEMS
Cavalier King Charles Spaniel – prone to elongated soft palate
Yorkshire Terrier – prone to incomplete tracheal cartilage rings
West Highland White Terrier – prone to emphysema following bronchitis

Disorders of the upper digestive tract

The dog's digestive system has a number of clearly defined sections. Each of these can be considered as a separate "food-processing" chamber with its own specific job. The mouth, oesophagus, stomach, liver, spleen and pancreas constitute the upper digestive tract, while the small and large intestines (gut), rectum and anus belong to the lower digestive tract. These all have their own special problems and are best considered separately.

> **SEE ALSO:**
> **Lower digestive tract disorders** see p.58
> **Treatment of vomiting and diarrhoea** see p.59.

Vomiting
One of the surest indications of digestive disorders is vomiting. All vomiting dogs should be assumed to have some form of inflammation in the system. (For treatment of vomiting, see p.59.)

Frequent vomiting is often a sign of *toxaemia* (poisoning by bacteria living in an affected part of the body) and may also be due to:
● Pyometra (see p.73)
● Liver or kidney failure (see pp.55 and 70)
● Foreign body blocking any part of the digestive tract.

Any problems involving frequent regurgitation of food should be investigated by a vet, since nasal damage can occur and food inhalation may cause lung damage. A vet will usually X-ray a dog with this type of problem for diagnosis prior to dealing with it surgically.

Problems of the stomach
Stomach or gastric disorders may be either acute (sudden, serious illness) or chronic (long-term, milder problem).

Signs of colic (stomach pain) include:
□ whimpering □ hunched position
□ tender abdomen when handled.
Acute disorders
Signs include: □ vomiting (often unproductive) □ dullness, with lack of appetite and colic □ thirst, but perhaps vomiting water □ vomiting soon after eating.
Chronic disorders
The major sign is intermittent vomiting at variable intervals after eating.
What is the treatment?
If you suspect a stomach disorder, consult your vet as soon as possible. Treatment requires accurate diagnosis; general treatment at home with kaolin preparations will alleviate vomiting prior to your dog seeing the vet.

Gastritis
Simple acute gastritis is a common problem in dogs. It can be thought of as a defence reaction which protects a dog from some of its own baser eating habits. Dogs are attracted to rank-smelling food, bones and poisons. Vomiting this material often avoids serious consequences, but don't bank on this if you see your dog eating something it shouldn't – contact a vet.

The major sign of gastritis is vomiting; if untreated, the dog may suffer from diarrhoea as well. Possible causes include:
● Swallowing poisons (see p.91)
● Ascarid worms (such as roundworm) living in the gut may move up into the stomach. If your dog vomits worms, this means others are present – so give it worming treatment (see p.62).
● Over-eating in puppies may trigger the vomiting reflex.
● Several specific infections cause gastritis, plus enteritis and other symptoms. These include canine distemper (see p.77), hepatitis (see p.56), parvovirus (see p.59) and leptospirosis (see pp. 56 and 71).

Gastric dilation or torsion

In gastric dilation, the stomach becomes inflated with gas. This is a veterinary emergency and may affect any breed. Gastric torsion occurs in deep-chested breeds when the stomach twists, trapping gas inside.

The cause of these problems is uncertain. It is possible that the "wrong" bacteria in the gut cause fermentation and inflation. Some greedy dogs swallow air with their food, and this, coupled with vigorous exercise after feeding, is thought to make stomach torsion more likely. Both these conditions make the stomach taut like a drum. The dog can't settle and is in great pain.

What is the treatment?
Unless treated quickly, the dog may die. The vet can often deflate a stomach dilation by inserting a tube into the dog's stomach, but the vast majority of gastric torsions require emergency surgery.

As a preventative measure, feed deep-chested dogs from a raised bowl and don't exercise them for at least one hour after feeding.

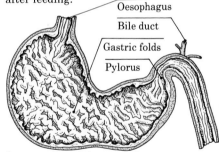

Oesophagus
Bile duct
Gastric folds
Pylorus

Cross-section of the stomach

The oesophagus

The most common oesophageal problems in dogs are associated with malformations of the oesophagus or related structures in the chest.

Vascular ring
Certain congenital disorders of the vessels of the heart can result in a "vascular ring" formed of blood vessels which encloses the oesophagus, preventing the dog from swallowing solids. Most congenital disorders produce the same signs which are:

☐ regurgitation soon after eating
☐ excessive salivation (drooling) due to failure to swallow ☐ coughing ☐ nasal discharge due to food going up the nose.

Obstruction in the oesophagus
A bone can lodge in the chest at the point where the oesophagus passes across the base of the heart or passes from the chest into the abdomen. Foreign bodies lodged at these points may need very delicate surgery to remove them through the chest. Sometimes a vet may be able to remove them with long forceps via incisions in the neck and stomach.

Problems of the pylorus

The pylorus (exit from the stomach) is another site where swallowed objects may stick. In addition, there exists a condition called *pyloric stenosis* where the sphincter, a valve which controls the flow from the stomach, is too powerful and prevents any solids leaving the stomach. This is most often seen in puppies being weaned and given their first solids, although it can also develop as a chronic problem in growing dogs.

The major sign is vomiting of solids; milky foods and fluids normally pass through. The only treatment for these conditions is surgery.

SPECIAL BREED PROBLEMS

Setters and Spaniels – prone to disorders of the pharynx muscles at the entrance to the oesophagus. These may fail to "grab" swallowed food
Scottish and West Highland White Terriers – prone to obstruction of the oesophagus with bones
Boxer – prone to gastric torsion, young dogs are particularly prone to pyloric stenosis
German Shepherd, Irish Setter, Weimaraner – prone to gastric torsion

Disorders of the mouth and teeth

The most common problems occurring inside a dog's mouth are due to new teeth not coming through and the accumulation of tartar. Luckily, dogs aren't especially prone to tooth decay. Affected teeth are usually molars (in old dogs) or ones cracked or damaged due to chewing bones or stones. Other problems can arise from the salivary glands which function in the dog's mouth.

Signs of problems include:
□ temporary teeth not falling out
□ worn, loose or broken teeth □ excess tartar □ halitosis (bad breath) □ pain on eating □ excess salivation □ gingivitis.

All these disorders need your vet's attention. Temporary teeth which show no signs of falling out should be removed. (Tooth retention is a fairly common problem with puppies, especially in toy breeds.) Broken or worn teeth can be capped or may need removing. Accumulated tartar should be removed by your vet or it will cause gingivitis (see below.) Loose teeth usually occur through neglect of accumulated tartar, causing gingivitis. If not extracted, they'll cause pain and more gingivitis.

SEE ALSO:
Dental problems of elderly dogs see p.86.

Canine dentistry
The most common procedures are tooth removal or scaling (tartar removal). Some vets may carry out fillings and cappings, but often, a vet will ask a local dentist to help out.

Gingivitis
Red, inflamed gums usually result from accumulation of tartar causing them to recede and allowing bacteria to invade. In some cases, temporary teeth not falling out when they should cause the permanent teeth to be damaged.

Malar abscess
The signs of this problem are seen on the face. An abscess on the roots of the carnassial tooth causes pain and swelling in front of and below the eye. Consult a vet without delay. Treatment usually involves removal of the tooth and antibiotics to treat the swelling.

Swelling on the tongue
If the salivary ducts beneath the tongue become blocked, a large, fluid swelling appears under one side of the tongue. This is a *ranula* (Latin meaning "frog-belly") and should be drained by the vet. The cause of the blockage should also be removed – it may be a *calculus* (stone) or even a grass seed. Consult a vet as soon as convenient.

PREVENTING TOOTH DECAY

The soft foods we feed our dogs tend to encourage tartar on the teeth, since there is less need for the chewing that helps to remove tartar as it forms. However, rawhide chews, large bones, hard biscuits or suitable toys (see p.17) are all safe items you can give your dog to chew.

Humans rely on cleaning their teeth to preve ..ecay. If you begin early, you can accustom your dog to having its teeth cleaned, too. Use a new toothbrush (keep this solely for your dog), and brush the teeth exactly as you would your own. Don't use toothpaste – dogs hate the taste. It is easiest to place small dogs on a table. Ask someone to hold the dog's head; you may need to use a muzzle (see p.89). If tartar has already built up, have it removed by the vet.

Disorders of the liver and spleen

The largest single organ in the body of all animals, the liver is a vitally important "chemical factory". The dog's liver performs several functions which are linked to the blood, food storage and the removal of toxins (poisons). Ridding the body of poisonous substances is the most important role. In doing this, it often becomes damaged by these substances. The *spleen* is close to the stomach and its main function is storage and re-cycling of red blood cells.

The general term for liver disease is "hepatitis". This can be acute (sudden and serious) or chronic (long-term and milder). Various diseases can affect the dog's liver including the major infectious diseases *leptospirosis* and *canine viral hepatitis* (see p.56). Problems in other parts of the body may also affect the liver – tumours in other areas of the abdomen, heart disease (see p.74) and hormonal problems.

The signs of liver disease are often vague and variable. This is partly due to the liver's capacity and its ability to repair itself; chronic (long-term) liver disease is often accompanied by repair. More than 80 percent of the liver needs to be destroyed before it fails completely.

Acute liver disease
The signs of this may vary greatly; it may be the culmination of a period of chronic disease. Possible signs include: □ abdominal pain, making the dog dull □ lack of appetite □ vomiting □ high temperature (almost always) □ jaundice (yellowness in gums and whites of eyes) □ haemorrhages in the gums □ pale faeces and dark urine.
What is the treatment?
If your dog shows a combination of these symptoms, don't delay – consult a vet immediately, even at night. The chances of recovery from acute liver disease are poor and delay reduces them still further. For diagnosis, the vet will need to take blood samples and possibly X-rays.

Treatment involves:
● Antibiotics to kill any bacterial infections
● Steroids to build up tissues
● Vitamins
● Intravenous fluids
● Strict dietary control.

Chronic liver disease
This is hard to define and diagnose. It may be the long-term sequel to attacks of acute liver disease, and can affect the brain. Possible signs include: □ weight loss, with or without a poor appetite □ bouts of dullness □ vomiting □ diarrhoea □ increased thirst □ dropsy (swelling of the belly) □ pale faeces □ apparent stupidity □ fits □ pressing the head on the wall or floor.
What is the treatment?
The long-term outlook is very poor; follow your vet's advice. Treatment is aimed at making the dog's life more comfortable. Its diet must be strictly controlled – if its brain isn't affected the dog should have high carbohydrate and low fat levels, combined with good-quality, highly digestible protein like eggs, cheese and meat. But if the brain *is* affected, a low-protein diet is called for. The dog needs steroids, possibly cortisone and vitamin supplements – B complex and Vitamin K.

Spleen tumour
Although tumours of the spleen are quite common, many are benign and cause no problems. If tumours spontaneously haemorrhage into the abdomen, filling it with blood, the dog may die within half an hour from an internal haemorrhage. But minor bleeding may cause nothing more than slight weakness.

The signs of spleen tumours are: □ abdominal swelling □ sudden weakness □ pale gums. Fortunately, if detected early enough, the spleen can be removed, other organs taking over its duties, and the dog can live a normal life.

Infectious canine hepatitis

Also known as Rubarth's disease, this highly contagious disease is caused by a virus. The main sufferers are young dogs, under one year of age. For this reason all young puppies should be vaccinated at around eight to ten weeks (see p.49). The incubation period for the disease is five to seven days.

What are the signs?

Initially, signs are vague. Dogs with only mild cases may simply go off their food and show a raised temperature for a few days. More severe cases become very dull, refuse to eat and are thirsty, but occasionally, a dog will die without warning. Common signs are: ☐ vomiting, with blood seen in the vomit in the later stages ☐ diarrhoea, which may also contain blood ☐ abdominal pain and restlessness ☐ excitability ☐ lack of coordination of the hind legs ☐ convulsions ☐ jaundice (occasionally) ☐ pale gums, with minute haemorrhages.

Other associated problems include kidney damage (this is the last part of the body to become clear of the virus). Recovered dogs shed live virus in their urine for months after infection, which makes them a serious risk to unvaccinated dogs. About 20 percent of dogs show some degree of "blue eye" (see p.68) after infection.

What is the treatment?

Veterinary treatment is essential – your vet may use steroids, antibiotics, transfusions, fluid therapy and kaolin-type preparations.

PREVENTING INFECTIOUS CANINE HEPATITIS

The only way of preventing infectious canine hepatitis is by vaccination. Once a dog has the disease, treatment is limited to relieving symptoms as they occur.

Two types of vaccine are available, living and dead. Live vaccines use a strain of the virus which has been modified so that it doesn't cause disease, and gives lifelong immunity.

However, dead vaccines are more commonly used because they don't produce the undesirable side-effects of some live vaccines (possible kidney damage and "blue eye" reactions).

Leptospirosis

Leptospira icterohaemorrhagiae is one of the two types of leptospirosis in dogs. The bacterium attacks the liver and is also the cause of Weil's disease in man (although dogs aren't thought to be a serious cause of infection). The second form affects the kidney (see p.71). Both are spread through infected urine and the incubation period is about one week. All puppies should be vaccinated.

The acute liver damage is often followed by death which can be rapid or take several days. Signs are: ☐ sudden dullness ☐ high temperature ☐ vomiting with thirst ☐ bloody diarrhoea ☐ jaundice (yellowness in gums and whites of eyes) ☐ small haemorrhages on the gums.

What is the treatment?

Consult a vet immediately. The bacteria do respond to antibiotics, so if treatment is prompt, there's a chance of recovery. Possible additional treatments include:
- Fluid therapy
- Drugs to stop vomiting
- Intestinal sedatives
- Blood transfusions

Observe normal hygiene precautions and wear rubber gloves when handling an affected dog.

SPECIAL BREED PROBLEMS

German Shepherd – prone to spleen tumour

Irish Setter – prone to hepatitis

Disorders of the pancreas

The pancreas performs two vital functions. It produces insulin which helps the body obtain energy from glucose. This is known as an *endocrine* process. The pancreas also produces digestive enzymes – an *exocrine* process. Both functions can be affected by disease. The most well-known exocrine disorder is E.P.I. and the most well-known endocrine disorder is diabetes.

Exocrine pancreatic insufficiency

Also known as E.P.I., this disorder means that the pancreas isn't fully formed. The exocrine section may be reduced or missing. This is usually a congenital problem, and may not become evident until later in a dog's life.

Dogs with this disorder can't digest food properly. They may try to eat their own faeces (because these still smell of food). Signs include: ☐ failure to put on weight ☐ bulky faeces (due to undigested food retaining water) ☐ pallor (due to undigested fat) ☐ dry, scurfy coat due to lack of oil.

What is the treatment?
Veterinary help is needed for a positive diagnosis by checking the enzyme levels in fresh faeces. Treatment requires permanent regular provision of enzymes (mainly trypsin) in tablet or powder form. (Unfortunately these are expensive in the long-term, and many dogs end up being euthanazed.) Special highly digestible oil supplements may be used; these include coconut and safflower oils. In addition, vitamin supplements will also be required.

Diabetes mellitus

The more common of the two types of diabetes is *diabetes mellitus*. More common in bitches, this is caused by the pancreas not producing enough insulin.

Insulin acts on the cells of the body to help them take glucose out of the blood for energy. The different organs in the body of a diabetic dog find it hard to get enough glucose unless levels in the blood are very high. When this happens (particularly after meals), the glucose "spills over" through the kidney filtration system, drawing water with it. Signs include: ☐ heavy thirst ☐ hunger ☐ tiredness ☐ weight loss.

What is the treatment?
All suspect cases should be taken to the vet for blood and urine tests. In mild cases, treatment may be possible by control of the diet alone, reducing levels of carbohydrate and fat. High fibre is important in a diabetic diet to help the dog absorb glucose more evenly. Oral drugs can stimulate production of insulin by the pancreas.

However, most diabetic dogs need regular insulin injections, given at home. There are several different types and dose regimes. Your vet will choose the most appropriate for your dog. You'll be shown how to give the injections and how to use the special kits for monitoring glucose in urine. It is important to stick to the prescribed routine.

Hypoglycaemic coma
Your dog will remain stable under given circumstances but if a feed is missed, the injected insulin has no glucose to "work on" and could cause a hypoglycaemic (low-glucose) coma with collapse and convulsions (see p.90). Too much exercise or activity could produce the same result. Keep honey or glucose syrup to give orally for emergencies. If diabetes remains untreated, highly toxic chemicals (ketones) may accumulate in the blood, with possibly fatal results.

SPECIAL BREED PROBLEMS

German Shepherd – prone to exocrine pancreatic insufficiency
Dachshund, King Charles Spaniel, poodles, Scottish Terrier – prone to diabetes

Disorders of the lower digestive tract

The lower section of the dog's digestive tract encompasses the gut (small and large intestines), duodenum, rectum and anus. As food passes through these areas, digestion continues and much of its water content is reabsorbed. The main signs of problems and diseases are:
□ vomiting □ diarrhoea □ straining. Some dogs have problems establishing the correct bacteria in their gut. This may be due to being given antibiotics but may also occur for no apparent reason. Worms in the small intestine (see p.62) can also cause problems, including fits.

SEE ALSO:
Disorders of the upper digestive tract see pp.52–3.

Acute small-intestine problems
The two acute (sudden, serious) problems which occur most commonly in the small intestine are a lodged foreign body and a condition called intussusception. Both are serious emergencies, needing urgent surgery. If they occur, don't delay – consult a vet immediately.
Foreign body in small intestine
If a foreign body passes through the stomach (perhaps after sitting there for weeks causing a chronic gastritis (see p.52) and occasional vomiting) it may fail to pass through the narrow small intestine where it sticks tight. Signs include: □ acute vomiting □ dullness □ colic □ apparent constipation.
Intussusception
This condition can cause the same symptoms in young dogs as a foreign body. The small intestine turns in on itself and the peristalsis process that moves food along drags a section of intestine inside the next section, producing a blockage. The trapped section of bowel often loses its blood supply and dies; it must be surgically corrected urgently.

Chronic small-intestine problems
Some of the chronic (long-term) disorders which fall into this category are difficult to diagnose and treat. Sometimes a partial obstruction may be caused by a swallowed piece of string or cloth. If these lodge, they can cause telescoping of sections of the bowel and ulceration, even peritonitis.

Signs include: □ occasional vomiting and/or diarrhoea □ persistent diarrhoea □ weight loss and variable appetite □ poor coat condition □ bouts of colic. Any condition causing blockage of the intestine requires surgical treatment.

Large-intestine problems
The large intestine (colon) is affected by similar diseases to those which attack the small intestine – tumours, leukaemia, foreign bodies, parasites, and inflammation of uncertain causes. The signs are: □ straining □ production of frequent small amounts of diarrhoea, often containing mucus and/or blood.

One group of large-intestine problems involves the build-up of food in the gut. This may be simple dietary constipation (see p.60) or may be associated with pain from one of the nearby organs, making defecation painful – anal sac problems (see p.60), prostatic disease (see p.73), fracture of the pelvis (see p.79) or arthritis (see p.78).

Occasionally the colon becomes weak and "balloons", encouraging accumulation of faeces. This condition is called "megacolon". It may be congenital, due to chronic colitis, or linked with the development of a perineal hernia, a section of the colon stretching the muscle in the pelvis and eventually producing a swelling on either or both sides of the anus.
What is the treatment?
Treatment of some of the non-specific colitis cases is often long-term and involves drugs. Specific treatment is also needed for infections.

VOMITING AND DIARRHOEA

Most causes of vomiting are linked with gastritis and most of diarrhoea with enteritis. If untreated, either is likely to lead to the other. If your dog is obviously ill or has a temperature more than 1°C above normal (38.5°C), consult a vet as soon as convenient.

Treatment for vomiting

In the absence of more serious signs (see p.41), starve the dog for 24 hours (puppies for 12 hours). Water should be continually available, but only in small amounts – 50–100 ml for small dogs, 200 ml for large dogs. If your dog drinks the whole ration, give the same amount in 30 minutes time, not immediately.

Provided the vomiting stops, give a small meal of light, easily digested food, such as scrambled egg. If the vomiting was frequent initially, it can help to mix a little brandy into this first meal – one teaspoon for a large dog, less for smaller breeds. If this is accepted with no further vomiting, give chicken, lean meat or white fish. Cook it and feed it moistened, mixed with boiled rice. Give this to your dog warm or cold. Feed three small meals a day rather than one large one. The next day, introduce more normal food if all is well, but keep amounts small. It is best to take a day or two to get fully back to normal in terms of quantity. You should only feed about two-thirds of the normal amount for the first four days.

Treatment for diarrhoea

Follow the same routine as for vomiting, but omit the scrambled egg, going straight to small meals of chicken, white fish or lean meat as above. Keep the dog on this diet until the diarrhoea improves, then re-introduce the normal diet. If the diarrhoea recurs, start again, introducing one normal diet ingredient at a time (to see if any of them is causing the problem).

Giving drugs

Your vet won't prescribe antibiotics for simple cases of gastroenteritis. Aluminium hydroxide suspensions are good gastric sedatives for vomiting dogs – one teaspoon three times a day for small dogs, one dessertspoon four times a day for large ones. Kaolin and morphine or kaopectate can also be given to dogs suffering from vomiting or diarrhoea (doses as for aluminium hydroxide). Keep one of these handy.

Parvovirus

A relatively new disease, parvovirus has been prevalent only since 1978 when it swept simultaneously across Britain, North America and Australia. This major viral disease of dogs is similar to panleukopaenia in cats.
What are the signs?
In most cases, the major signs are: □ a severe enteritis with haemorrhagic diarrhoea □ acute vomiting, even of fluids □ severe depression □ high temperature. Unless treated promptly, the disease can be fatal. In the initial outbreak, death was common despite treatment and there is still a possibility that an affected dog may succumb.
What is the treatment?
Protection hinges on vaccination. This should be given to all puppies (see p.49) and should be followed up with routine annual boosters.

Treatment is symptomatic. This disease is often acute and dramatic therapy may be needed – fluid given via drips and blood transfusions plus antibiotic cover to avoid secondary infection. Contact your vet immediately you suspect it.

Constipation

One of the most common problems in elderly dogs and those that eat bones is constipation. If you notice it early, before your dog becomes dull and ill and loses its appetite through toxicity, constipation can often be treated at home. The early signs are: ☐ straining ☐ very hard faeces ☐ tail raised for defecation ☐ anus bulging. If your dog is completely unable to pass faeces, contact your vet.

What is the treatment?

If your dog *is* passing faeces, but with difficulty, help it by giving liquid paraffin (one tablespoon twice daily for a 10–15 kg dog, increasing up to two tablespoons twice daily for a dog 30 kg or more). This should lubricate the bowel and soften any blockage. If it doesn't sort out the problem within two days, or if your dog becomes ill, contact the vet.

If the problem recurs, contact the vet. Your dog may have a problem such as a rectal tumour or an enlarged prostate. Elderly dogs that are prone to constipation can be eased by giving bran in the diet – two teaspoons daily for 10–15 kg dogs, increasing to a handful for dogs of 30 kg and over.

RECTAL PROLAPSE

This is a veterinary emergency and occasionally occurs after very severe, untreated diarrhoea or with constipation or rectal tumours. The rectum pops out like an inside-out sleeve and you'll see a lump ranging from the size of a cherry to a bright red sausage hanging out of the dog's rectum. If you notice this, contact the vet immediately. Treatment involves pushing the rectum back through the central hole. If it is a small prolapse you may be able to treat it yourself before getting to the vet but if you can't see the central hole, don't waste time looking. Delay could result in major surgery to remove a section of the rectum.

Action

1 Get the dog to the surgery immediately.

2 Meanwhile, keep the lump moist with cotton wool soaked in warm water.

3 If it is a small prolapse you may be able to treat it yourself before getting to the vet (see above).

EMPTYING THE ANAL SACS

Occasionally, a dog's anal ducts become blocked and the anal sacs need emptying. They may be swollen and painful. You might notice your dog licking the area repeatedly or "scooting" along the ground. Always have the sacs emptied by a vet the first time. If you'd like to try doing it yourself the next time it happens, ask the vet to show you exactly how.

The anal sacs are positioned at 4 o'clock and 8 o'clock either side of the anus, with their ducts leading to the anal rim. The aim is to get your fingers partially behind them and squeeze out the contents. In some dogs, this is difficult or impossible without hurting them. Take these dogs to the vet who may perform the task "internally".

The most acceptable method for dog owners is the external method.

You'll need a helper to restrain the dog. Take the precaution of tying its nose, too (see p.279).

Hold a pad of cotton wool across the palm of one hand and raise the dog's tail with the other. Apply the pad to the rear of the dog. With the middle finger and thumb either side of the anus, squeeze inwards (towards the anus) and outwards so that the contents of the glands are forced out.

Nutritional disorders

Feeding your dog correctly is one of the most crucial aspects of keeping it healthy. Several important diseases are probably due in part to improper nutrition, including hip dysplasia (see p.79). The wrong diet may result in:
● Underfeeding, resulting in lack of energy, loss of weight and starvation.
● Overfeeding, resulting in excess energy, weight gain, and obesity.
● Deficiency diseases, caused by a lack of specific components in the diet.
● Toxicity, caused by an excess of a particular ingredient, such as a vitamin or a mineral.

> **SEE ALSO:**
>
> **Dietary needs** see pp.32–3.
> **Reducing diet for obese dogs** see p.37.

Nutritional bone diseases

Rickets is caused by a deficiency of Vitamin D. The dog can't use calcium properly and its bones become weak and bend, whilst the joints enlarge. It is seen in dogs that grow rapidly, but receive no supplementation in their diet.
Osteoporosis is caused by a diet low in calcium or high in phosphorus (such as an all-meat diet). The bones appear normal but are weak and break easily. The calcium/phosphorus ratio is very important in any dog's diet (see p.32).

Hypertrophic osteodystrophy (bone scurvy) is a strange disease, seen particularly in giant breeds. Bone scurvy causes pain and swelling around the growth plates of long bones. It is thought this may be caused by lack of Vitamin C, due to rapid growth and over-supplementation with Vitamin D.

A proper diet should prevent these diseases occurring, but seek veterinary advice if you suspect any of the conditions in your dog. Veterinary treatment may involve giving vitamins intravenously and special diets.

Obesity

This is unfortunately a common problem in pet dogs and is due to an excess of food. The normal distribution of fat on a dog's body includes a thin layer under the skin, other layers between the muscles of the abdominal wall, and some deposits in the abdomen. Except in fit, smooth-coated breeds you probably won't notice the ribs but they should be felt easily; a fat layer of more than 5 mm over the ribs suggests the start of obesity.

Be aware of obesity in your dog and try to avoid it. Surplus weight
● Can cause osteoarthritis (see p.78)
● Makes veterinary examination difficult
● Adds risks for anaesthetics and surgery.

The breeds most at risk from obesity seem to be: Cocker Spaniels, Labradors, terriers, collies, poodles and dachshunds.

TREATING OBESITY

The only way to treat an overweight dog is to give it less to eat. Increasing exercise levels helps but isn't the complete answer. A home-cooked reducing diet is outlined in the *Feeding* chapter (see p.37). In addition, follow these principles:
● No biscuit
● No fats
● Use an all-meat canned food instead of a complete canned diet
● Use bran as a filler
● Include cooked vegetables as fillers
● Try a complete canned "obesity diet" (available from your vet on prescription)
● Give dieting dogs a course of a proprietary multivitamin preparation.

Parasites

Canine parasites fall into two groups: ectoparasites (those which live on the outside of the dog) such as ringworm, lice, fleas and ticks, and endoparasites (those which live inside the dog) including roundworms, hookworms, whipworms and tapeworms.

Most ectoparasites can be treated with suitable insecticidal sprays and shampoos. Good grooming and a clean environment will also protect your dog from fleas. Wash its bedding regularly.

SEE ALSO:
Heartworm see p.75

Worming

Regular worming is essential both for the health of your dog, and to protect the family from the slight risk from one particular worm called *Toxocara*. Your vet will advise on safety and effectiveness of the preparations available.

Puppies should be treated for roundworms every 2 weeks from 4 weeks of age up to 6 months of age. After that, every dog should be wormed every 6 months. Pregnant bitches need a special worming routine. Tapeworms are less of a danger to children, but all dogs should be tapewormed every 6 months, and more regularly should segments be seen in the stools. As a matter of habit, it is good hygiene to clear up dog faeces as soon as possible from the garden.

Ringworm

Ringworm is an infectious fungus which grows on the skin and within the coat. Signs are: □ weak, broken hairs □ irritated, scaly, inflamed skin.
What is the treatment?
It is important to seek veterinary advice as this parasite can infect humans. Treatment can take the form of special iodine shampoos, clipping the affected area, creams, and a drug given by mouth.

Lice

There are two types of louse – biting lice which chew on skin flakes, and sucking lice which cause more irritation because they penetrate the skin to feed on tissue fluids. (Neither will spread to cats or people.) Lice are grey, about 2mm long and lay small eggs (nits) which stick to the dog's hairs.

Give repeat treatments of insecticide sprays or baths (at least three at five to seven day intervals) to kill the adults and any hatching larvae.

Fleas

Fleas can act as intermediate hosts for other dog parasites, but the major problem they cause is skin irritation. When a flea bites, it injects saliva to stop the blood clotting whilst it sucks it up. The saliva contains chemicals which often cause an allergic reaction in the dog. The signs are: □ bites looking like small red pimples □ black, gritty material in the coat. In some hypersensitive dogs, flea saliva triggers off large areas of inflammation on the animal's back.
What is the treatment?
Flea control will only work if the dog's environment is treated, so you should spring-clean the house and treat the dog's favourite places with a suitable insecticidal spray. Flea collars are a good extra precaution, alternatively spray badly affected animals frequently with insecticide throughout the summer months (the flea season).

Ticks

The common tick seen on dogs is the sheep tick. This has a large abdomen that stretches as it fills with blood. It hangs on to the dog's hair and sticks its mouth parts through the skin to suck blood. Ticks are usually found on the underside of the dog, under the forelegs and on the head.
What is the treatment?

Try to remove every tick when you see it. It is important to extract the head, otherwise an abscess may form. If the head is left in, warm compresses help draw out the infection, combined with antibacterial washes and creams.

Removing a tick

There are various ways of removing ticks, none of them completely foolproof. A good method is to get the tick's head to relax or die by dabbing it with alcohol (such as gin or methylated spirits). Wait a couple of minutes, then use fine-pointed tweezers to extract the tick. Grasp it near (*not* on) the mouth parts. A sharp jerk usually dislodges the tick.

Alternatively, flea sprays can be used locally on ticks. The tick will then die and can be removed the following day. Regular use of a flea spray in tick areas often keeps them away.

Roundworms

Several of these parasites affect dogs but the most important ones belong to the *Ascarid* family. *Toxocara canis* and *Toxascaris leonina* both live in the small intestine. Other roundworms infest the large intestine, blood vessels and respiratory tract.

Ascarids feed on digesting food in the dog's gut, and are particularly harmful to puppies. They penetrate a puppy's gut wall and pass via the blood to the liver and then the lungs. From there they crawl up the trachea to be coughed up and swallowed, again ending up in the gut. Infected puppies may develop:
☐ hepatitis ☐ pneumonia ☐ fits

☐ obstruction in the gut.

As the puppy gets older most of the worms travel to the muscles, where they form cysts. These lie dormant until the puppy (if it is a bitch) becomes pregnant, when they migrate to the embryo puppies' lungs. Thus, virtually every puppy is born with roundworm, and must be wormed frequently.

How roundworms affect humans

These worms can infect humans, and in a very low number of cases, cause disease. Very rarely, they become encysted in a child's eye, when the eye may have to be removed. Good hygiene and common sense concerning children and puppies should control the problem.

Hookworms and whipworms

Both hookworms and larger whipworms are blood suckers. Both types are visible to the naked eye. These worms can cause anaemia (see p.75), diarrhoea or poor condition.

Tapeworms

The most common dog tapeworm is *Dipylidium caninum*. It is transmitted by fleas in which its larvae develop. Segments of *Dipylidium* are like wriggling rice grains. They tickle the anus and may cause discomfort.

What is the treatment?

Modern tapeworm treatments eliminate all types and your vet will advise on frequency of use. If you see any worm segments in your dog's faeces, treat it as soon as possible. Spray the dog and the house for fleas.

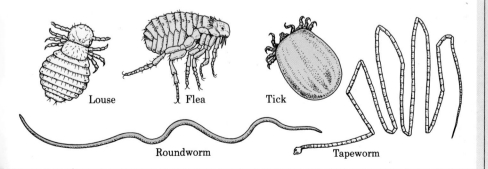

Louse Flea Tick

Roundworm Tapeworm

Ear disorders

The dog's ears are incredibly sensitive and can detect very high-frequency sounds inaudible to man. Although the outer ear (ear flap) varies so much between breeds, the structure and function of the middle and inner ears is the same for every dog. It is important to watch your dog for signs of ear disease. Your vigilance can help prevent the spread of infection to the middle and inner ears, and you should know how to examine the ears and how to apply any medicaments. Periodical ear cleaning should be undertaken with care. For the proper method of doing this, see p.66.

Examining the ears

Carry out a routine examination of your dog's ears every month – more frequently if it has had any recent ear problems. Establishing this routine makes treatment much easier for you, the dog and the vet.

1 Place the dog on a table (if it is small enough); leave larger dogs on the floor. Restrain the dog (see p.82).

2 Lift the ear flap and look down the canal (a torch may help). Inside the ear canal, you should see a clean surface, similar to the skin on the hairless part of the dog's belly. A little wax is no problem

---

DISCHARGE FROM THE EAR

A discharge indicates an infection of the outer ear (*otitis externa*).

Things to look for
- Gritty, black material
- Runny, smelly black discharge
- Thick yellow/green discharge
- Pain
- Ear-flap swelling
- Apparent deafness

Possible causes
Depending on the discharge, the cause could be mites (gritty discharge), yeasts (runny, black discharge) or bacterial infections (thick, yellow discharge).

Treatment
These conditions should be examined and treated by the vet with appropriate medication. Mites: antiparasitic preparation. Yeasts: preparation containing antifungal drugs. Bacterial infections: antibiotics.

Urgency
✚✚✚ Don't delay – consult a vet immediately.

SWOLLEN EAR FLAP

A swelling on the inside of the ear flap (small or covering the whole surface) is likely to be an *aural haematoma* (a blood blister formed due to haemorrhage inside the ear flap), often caused by vigorous head shaking.

Things to look for
- Dog shaking its head
- Repeated pawing at the ear
- Tilting the head
- One ear flap at a different angle
- Soft, fluid swellings on inside of ear flap

Possible causes
- Blow to the ear
- Ear infection causing head shaking
- Fighting

Treatment
Clean the ear (see p.66) and if there's a delay in seeing the vet, bind it to the head with a clean bandage. Surgery is needed to reduce scarring and prevent a "cauliflower ear".

Urgency
✚✚ Consult a vet as soon as convenient.

and should be left alone, but if wax or a hair plug is blocking the ear, it needs plucking and/or cleaning.

3 Smell the ear. A healthy ear has a warm, waxy smell. An unpleasant or strong odour suggests an infection requiring veterinary advice.

4 Reward the dog by making a fuss of it.

Common ear problems
Watch for problems if you own a dog with long ear flaps (such as a Basset) or one with heavy hair growth on large flaps (like a Cocker Spaniel). These flaps reduce ventilation, leading to overheating and excess wax which goes "off" and becomes infected.

Some breeds, such as poodles, have narrow ear canals and are prone to accumulation of wax. Even breeds with wide ear canals and not too much hair in the ears may suffer occasionally from excess wax.

All dogs have hair in their ears which can cause overheating and infection by forming a plug which blocks the ear canal. Remove this by plucking it out with your fingers. Most of the live hair will remain, but dead hair should come out. The ear canal should be clear down the centre as far as you can see. If the opening is still obstructed, you should trim hair away carefully with round-ended scissors.

PAINFUL EARS
There are a variety of causes of painful ears.

Things to look for
- Purulent discharge
- Black waxy material
- Excess hair
- Swelling on ear flap
- Tilting or shaking the head
- Pawing at the ears
- Head painful to touch

Possible causes
- Ear infection
- Excess wax or hair
- Foreign body
- Aural haematoma (see below left)

Treatment
For treatment of discharge, see left.

Accumulated wax and hair should be removed (see *Cleaning the ears*, p.66). Dab calamine lotion on any red areas to soothe pain but don't pour it down the ear.

If the ear looks clean but the dog is in sudden distress, this suggests a foreign body which should be removed by your vet. Don't introduce anything into the ear, even oil.

Urgency
+++ If there is any inflammation or discharge, don't delay – consult a vet immediately.

POOR HEARING
Deafness is uncommon in dogs but infections may temporarily impair hearing.

Things to look for
- Lack of response to calls for food, walks
- Pain, scratching, head tilt
- Discharge

Possible causes
- Chronic disease blocking outer ear
- Blockage of the ear canal by wax
- Inner-ear infection
- Congenital disorder
- Genetic cause – the same genes which produce albinos can cause deafness

Treatment
Remove any wax or hair blocking the ear canal and have any infections which are present treated by the vet.

Urgency
++ If you suspect infection, consult a vet as soon as convenient.

CLEANING THE EARS

First check the ears for hair plugs. If necessary, pluck out any dead hair with your fingers. Then remove excess wax with an oily cleanser – warm cod-liver oil, liquid paraffin or a special ear cleaner. Don't use powders – they can make matters worse.

Ear cleaning must not be too vigorous or frequent. The ear produces wax partly in response to irritation; too much cleaning causes just that.

Warning When cleaning your dog's ears, never poke the tip of a cotton bud out of sight You'll do no harm if you keep it in view. Use your fingers as a stop and hold it like a pencil, just above the "bulb".

1 Introduce the oil well down the ear canal using a dropper, then massage around the base of the ear flap to spread it. Look to see if any oil or wax has come to the surface.

2 If it has, remove it with cotton buds or cotton wool. If you see no blood and the dog isn't in distress, continue cleaning until no more wax comes up.

APPLYING EAR MEDICINES

Don't use powders unless given them by the vet – since they can cake. Thick ointments "gum up" the ear, reducing ventilation and obscuring visible signs. Use proprietary drops, cod-liver oil, medicinal liquid paraffin or prescribed medicines.

1 Hold the ear flap to steady the head. Introduce the dropper or tube nozzle carefully into the ear. Squeeze in the prescribed dose.

2 Allow the medicine to run down the inside of the ear, then massage the ear canal from the outside to distribute it.

Eye disorders

The structure of a dog's eye is much like a human's, but there are a few features which can cause problems for dogs, such as the lacrimal duct or the third eyelid.

It is very important to notice any problems in dog's eyes early. Seek veterinary advice immediately for all eye disorders. Irrigating the eye (see p.69) may relieve discomfort until your dog can see the vet.

Congenital canine eye defects are unfortunately common. They can be extremely painful and you should never breed from dogs with such disorders.

SEE ALSO:
Bandaging the eye see p.93.
Foreign body in eye see p.91.

DISCHARGE FROM THE EYE

The veterinary term for discharge from the eyes is *epiphora*. It is the most common sign of eye disease.

A clear discharge suggests a problem relating to drainage of tears. It can also be caused by irritation and inflammations like conjunctivitis. If the discharge becomes cloudy or *purulent* (thick and discoloured), the eye is probably infected.

Things to look for
● Clear or purulent discharge
● Swelling
● Pain

Possible causes
● Blocked tear ducts
● Conjunctivitis (see p.68)
● Glaucoma (see p.68)
● General infections such as distemper (see p.77)

Treatment
Don't allow hair round the eye to become matted or the discharge to accumulate – a sure way to cause infection.

Until you take the dog to the vet's, bathe the area round the eyes using lint gauze soaked in warm water or a proprietary eye wash.

In the case of blocked tear ducts, the vet will need to flush these out under anaesthetic or enlarge the openings. For treatment of conjunctivitis and glaucoma see p.68.

Urgency
✚✚ If the discharge is clear, consult a vet as soon as convenient.
✚✚✚ If the discharge is purulent or the dog is in pain, don't delay – consult a vet immediately.

SWOLLEN EYE

Swelling in the tissues behind the eye can push the eye forward. The eyeball itself can also swell and be forced out of its socket.

Things to look for
● Protruding eyeball (compare it with the other)
● Glazed stare
● Dilated pupil (due to nerve damage)
● Lids unable to close

Possible causes
● Blow to the head
● Bleeding after a road accident
● Infection behind the eye
● Tumour
● Glaucoma (see p.68)

Urgency
✚✚✚ Any delay could cost the dog its eye – consult a vet immediately.

Blindness

A dog's excellent hearing combined with its memory of the floor-plan of your house may make blindness difficult to spot. A blind dog will manage very well if you are patient and understanding. It can go for walks as usual, but will probably stay close to you. Help by speaking to your dog frequently and not moving furniture around more than necessary. If you have to leave the dog alone in the house, the sound of a radio reduces its degree of isolation.

Third eyelid problems

In some breeds, such as the St Bernard and the Bloodhound, it is normal for the third eyelid to show, but in most dogs there's probably some problem if it suddenly becomes visible or protrudes.

Possible cause include: ☐ painful eye condition ☐ weight loss ☐ scrolled cartilage (a congenital deformity) ☐ prolapsed *nictitans gland* (most common in breeds with loose lower lids).

The signs of third eyelid problems include: ☐ a whitish membrane, usually with a black edge, protruding from the inner corner of the eye ☐ reddish, pea-shaped lump in the inner corner of eye ☐ foreign body behind third eyelid ☐ painful eye ☐ red eye.

If your dog develops these signs, contact a vet immediately. In the meantime, irrigate the eye to keep it moist.

Congenital eyelid and eyelash problems

The most common deformities of the eyelids are *entropion* and *ectropion*, both of which require surgical correction.

In entropion, the eyelid turns inwards, causing the lashes to dig into the surface of the eye. In ectropion the eyelid turns outwards. This causes tears to pool in the pouch formed by the lid, so that the cornea dries out.

A dog's eyelashes may grow in the wrong direction so that they rub on the eyes, causing pain and redness. This is called *trichiasis. Distichiasis* is a similar problem where extra hairs on the lid margin rub on the eye. If left untreated they may cause serious damage, even blindness. Fortunately the hairs can be removed by surgery or electrolysis.

Conjunctivitis

This is a painful condition in which the conjunctiva becomes inflamed. The cause may be an infection, a scratch, a congenital disorder, a tumour on the lid, or an irritant such as dust or smoke. Signs include: ☐ tears ☐ screwing up the eye ☐ redness.

If the cornea becomes inflamed *(keratitis)* it begins to look cloudy or even powder blue and completely opaque. This condition is seen in hepatitis (see p.56) and is called "blue eye". The white of the eye may then become severely congested. Finally, chronic inflammation can lead to a film of black pigment spreading across the eye.

If the cause of inflammation is treated in time, the condition can be halted or slowed. The black film can also sometimes be removed by delicate surgery.

Cataracts

These are opaque areas in the lens which can diminish a dog's vision. Some are hereditary whilst others may be caused by a dog's mother being ill or poorly fed during pregnancy. Many dogs develop cataracts in old age, but it isn't always necessary to treat them.

Glaucoma

This is a disorder involving the drainage system of the inside of the eye. It may be caused by: ☐ haemorrhage ☐ inflammation in the anterior chamber ☐ congenital defect. Fluids are continually produced within the eye to nourish it. If their drainage outlets become blocked, the fluids build up, making the globe stretch painfully. The eye becomes severely inflamed and pain makes the dog shed continual tears. Other signs include: ☐ swelling ☐ pain ☐ sensitivity to light.

If your dog develops these signs, contact a vet immediately. Treatment is surgical or involves special drugs to reduce fluid production, dilate the pupil and improve internal drainage.

Disorders of the retina
The light-sensitive retina can be affected by disease. The most serious involve abnormalities in the retinal structure.
Progressive retinal atrophy (P.R.A.)
In this disease the blood supply to sections of the retina gradually "withers away" and the light-sensitive cells die. The main sign is deteriorating vision. This disorder has two forms – central and generalized – which both lead to impairment of the vision. Central P.R.A. may not cause total blindness but generalized P.R.A. often does. Affected dogs may also have cataracts.
Collie eye anomaly (C.E.A.)
This strange congenital disorder affects collies and Shetland Sheepdogs. It can lead to retinal haemorrhage or detached retina, both of which can cause blindness. Some level of C.E.A. is present in a worryingly large percentage of collies. Fortunately only

about five percent of affected dogs go blind and then often only in one eye. The only solution is long-term screening of puppies for future breeding selection.

SPECIAL BREED PROBLEMS
Terriers – may be prone to luxation (dislocated lens)
German Shepherd – may be prone to conjunctivitis, scrolled cartilage, cataracts
St Bernard – may be prone to pro-lapsed nictitans, scrolled cartilage
Bloodhound, Boxer, Bulldog, Basset – may be prone to prolapsed nictitans
Collies – may be prone to Collie eye anomaly, central P.R.A.
Shetland Sheepdog – may be prone to Collie eye anomaly, central P.R.A.
Golden Retriever, Labrador – may be prone to central P.R.A., cataracts
Cairn Terrier, Cocker Spaniel, Dachshunds, Poodles, Irish Setter – may be prone to generalized P.R.A.
Afghan Hound, Boston Terrier, Poodles, Staffordshire Bull Terrier – may be prone to cataracts

IRRIGATING THE EYE

Any eye condition needs professional attention. Depending on the nature of the disorder, the veterinarian may recommend using an eye wash consisting of salty water.

1 Hold the eye open with your finger and thumb. Soak a pad of lint in the wash; squeeze over the eye.

2 If drops have been prescribed, tilt the head slightly and apply into the corner of each eye.

Urinary disorders

The part of the dog's urinary system most commonly affected by disease is the kidney. Kidney disease (known as *nephritis*) is a major cause of death in dogs, so consult the vet immediately you suspect it. Although the signs of individual diseases vary, general signs include: □ abdominal pain □ blood in urine □ swollen abdomen. Often, however, a problem is only noticed when renal (kidney) failure develops, which may be acute (sudden and serious), or chronic (long-term).

Acute kidney failure

Signs are: □ dullness □ vomiting □ lack of appetite □ bad breath □ abdominal pain □ not passing urine. Possible causes are:
● Poisoning (see p.91)
● Acute infections such as leptospirosis (see p.71)
● Secondary to an infection such as pyometra (see p.73)
● Obstruction
● Paralysis of bladder
● Long-term chronic kidney problem.

What is the treatment?
Consult the vet immediately. He or she will use a blood test to assess the severity of the problem. Your dog may need antibiotics, fluid treatment, dialysis, vitamins or anti-emetics.

Chronic kidney failure

Signs vary and may include: □ excessive thirst □ passing a lot of urine □ mouth ulcers □ anaemia (see p.75) □ weight loss and muscle wasting □ bad breath. Possible causes are:
● Minor problems with several factors leading to acute failure
● Tumours (cancer)
● Congenital kidney disorder.
What is the treatment?
Consult your vet who will be able to give your dog steroids and fluid treatment and provide advice on home care. Put the dog on a low-protein diet (see *Special diets*, below) and give it plenty to drink.

To avoid kidney disease, try to ensure no chronic illnesses are allowed to go untreated and that your dog is vaccinated regularly against leptospirosis.

SPECIAL DIETS FOR DOGS WITH KIDNEY DISEASE

Many vets advise low protein diets for dogs with nephritis, to "reduce the strain on the kidneys". In fact, this is often in direct opposition to the needs of the body, which is crying out for good-quality protein. Unfortunately a damaged kidney leaks protein, and if this isn't supplied in the diet, the dog uses its own muscles as a source. Hence the wasting of dogs with chronic nephritis.

Begin restricting dietary protein only on the advice of your vet who can judge the severity of the disease through blood tests. In early cases the slightly reduced-protein "geriatric diet" (see p.37) is generally the most suitable. For dogs that leak vast amounts of protein and develop dropsy (swollen abdomen) and swollen legs a high protein, salt-free diet is needed, along with prescribed diuretics

from your vet.

Increase the rice content of the basic home-cooked diet (p.37) to $\frac{5}{6}$ teacupful and reduce the meat content to $\frac{1}{6}$ teacupful (about 40 g). To make the diet more tasty, add two teaspoons of chicken or turkey fat. Protein levels can be further reduced on your vet's advice by using one egg instead of each $\frac{1}{6}$ teacupful of meat. Eggs provide protein and are very digestible.

Diet supplements

To maintain a low level of phosphorus, substitute calcium carbonate for the bonemeal in the diet supplement. A little salt added to the food helps maintain thirst and kidney flow and compensates for sodium lost via the kidneys.

Other parts of the urinary system

Problems may occur in the lower urinary tract, particularly affecting the bladder and urethra.

Stones in ureter and bladder
Sometimes salts present in the urine crystalize out and form *calculi* or "stones". These rub on the lining of the bladder and cause irritation (*cystitis*, see below). Signs are: ☐ straining ☐ passing urine frequently ☐ blood in the urine.

What is the treatment?
These disorders need surgical treatment. Once your vet has confirmed that stones are present, they can be surgically removed.

Stones in urethra
In dogs rather than bitches the stones can become lodged in the urethra which carries the urine out of the body through the penis. This is painful. Signs are: ☐ straining ☐ vomiting ☐ lack of appetite.

Urgent veterinary treatment (usually surgery) is needed to remove the obstruction, otherwise back pressure may rupture the bladder or damage the kidney. At this point the pain may disappear but a build-up of toxins will kill the dog unless he is treated promptly.

Cystitis
Infections in the bladder can also cause cystitis, more commonly in bitches. Chronic cystitis can result in stone formation requiring surgery (see stones, above). In mild cases your vet will often prescribe a urinary acidifier such as Vitamin C or chlorethamine, to make the urine less alkaline and less suitable for bacteria to live in. Signs include:
☐ blood in urine ☐ frequent urination
☐ licking the penis or vulva.

Leptospirosis

One of the two forms of this bacterial disease, *Leptospira canicola*, attacks the dog's kidney. Like the liver-disease form (see p.56), the organism is spread through infected urine.

What are the signs?
Mild cases may simply be "off colour" for a couple of days. Serious cases may be very dull and vomit as they become uraemic (urea, a waste product in urine, accumulates in the blood due to kidney malfunction). Uraemic dogs often develop mouth ulcers and have bad breath. Later, abdominal colic sets in. Recovery from infection leaves scarring in the kidney and contributes to chronic kidney failure.

What is the treatment?
Have your dog vaccinated regularly. However, if you suspect it in your dog, don't delay – contact a vet immediately. He or she can give antibiotics to combat the bacteria, plus drugs to stop vomiting. Drips, dialysis and transfusions may also be needed, depending on severity.

Urinary incontinence

It is easy to distinguish an incontinent dog which leaks urine in the house from a scent-marking dog (behavioural problem) or one which simply isn't house-trained.

Many incontinent dogs leak urine whilst asleep, leaving a wet patch when they get up. There are several possible causes of incontinence:
● Ectopic ureters – a congenital condition. Puppies may be born with their ureters emptying directly into the urethra and out, rather than having urine pass first into the bladder. This can be corrected surgically.
● Urination during an epileptic fit (see p.90)
● Cystitis (see above)
● Prostate disease (see p.72)
● Old age (see p.86).

Reproductive disorders

Some problems affecting the dog's reproductive system, although annoying for breeders, aren't serious. However, other conditions can be life-threatening emergencies. Keep your eyes open for signs of trouble in both bitches and dogs.

Fertility and libido problems

Problems relating to fertility or libido can be complex. Apart from making sure your dog is otherwise in good health and within the normal weight range for its size and breed, there's little you can do.

Disorders of the male tract

Several problems can occur in the male dog's system. In general, consult the vet if you notice signs including: ☐ heavy discharge from the penis ☐ bleeding ☐ pain.

Inflammation of the sheath

Young dogs often suffer a mild inflammation on the inside of the sheath. The sign of this is a pale, greenish discharge. If mild, simply bathe off the discharge whenever you notice it.

If the discharge becomes excessive, consult your vet. The problem is caused by an infection at the root of the penis and treatment involves antibiotics given by mouth and antibiotic dressings.

Bleeding penis

Apart from accidental injury, possible causes of this are:
● Bitching injury – dog forced to dismount during mating
● Acute cystitis (see p.71)
● Prostate leaking blood.

Don't delay – take the dog to the vet immediately. If the problem is a bitching injury, he may have a V-shaped split and need an anaesthetic and some stitches. You can help in the meantime by applying a cold compress to the sheath. Use a towel or a large wad of cotton wool soaked in cold water or wrapped round some ice cubes. Press this tightly onto the sheath, wrap a bath towel round the dog and tie it firmly.

Paraphimosis

The swollen penis may be trapped by the sheath opening and unable to return to its normal size – a tourniquet effect. If the penis doesn't regain its usual size within 15 minutes, try the cold compress technique described above. If there's no response after a further 15 minutes, seek urgent veterinary advice. Surgery may be required to enlarge the opening of the sheath.

Cryptorchidism

Dogs that haven't been castrated but have only one or no testes present in the scrotum are known as "cryptorchids". The testes should descend through the inguinal canal into the scrotum during early puppyhood. It is difficult to be certain if a dog has a retained testis until about ten months of age. If, after this time, a testis has not descended, the vet will remove it surgically; retained testes are prone to cancer. Never use a cryptorchid dog for breeding.

Tumour in the testicles

These tumours may produce female hormones, resulting in odd effects in the male dog – symmetrical hair loss and occasionally, breast development and a pendulous sheath. Consult a vet as soon as convenient – testicle tumours should be surgically removed when spotted.

Prostate disease

The prostate gland is most prone to disease in old dogs. Tumours may develop, or more commonly, the gland becomes enlarged. This internal problem only manifests itself when the dog has problems passing faeces – pain due to the condition leads to constipation.

Any dog with problems or pain on passing faeces (see Constipation p.60) or blood in the urine should be taken to a vet immediately.

An enlarged prostate can be treated with female hormones (even tumours may partially respond to these). To make life easier for the dog, ensure there is always plenty of roughage in its diet.

Disorders of the female tract

A bitch's reproductive system is prone to various ills, many linked to fluctuations in hormone levels and changes that occur in the womb with each heat.

Signs that something is wrong include: ☐ abnormal discharges ☐ excessive thirst ☐ persistent bleeding or swelling ☐ nursing behaviour ☐ production of milk six to seven weeks after a heat.

Pregnancy
If your bitch has mated and you don't want puppies, the vet can inject her to prevent conception within the first 24–48 hours. If the mating was intentional, you probably won't see any signs for the first four weeks. Signs of pregnancy include: ☐ teats pink and enlarged ☐ embryos able to be felt (fifth week) ☐ loss of appetite ☐ slight vomiting of froth (fifth week) ☐ increased appetite (sixth week) ☐ definite alteration in body outline (seventh week).

Eclampsia
This serious condition (due to calcium deficiency) affects bitches just before whelping or in the first month of lactation. Signs include: ☐ restlessness ☐ panting ☐ whining ☐ stiffness ☐ twitching muscles ☐ lack of co-ordination ☐ convulsions ☐ eventual collapse.

If not treated, death will occur; consult the vet immediately you suspect it. Treatment involves calcium injections. Prevention is not certain, but proper vitamin and mineral supplements will help.

Pyometra
This means "pus in the womb". Infection usually occurs six to eight weeks after a heat. The bitch may be off-colour and develop: ☐ excessive thirst ☐ abnormal discharge, yellow, greenish, or reddish and thick ☐ dullness ☐ vomiting.

Suspicion of this condition should be reported immediately to your vet. Life-saving surgery is needed to remove the ovaries and womb (ovaro-hysterectomy). In some cases, drugs may settle the problem temporarily.

Ovarian cyst
The sign of this problem is persistent bleeding from the vulva (a thin, light red discharge) after a heat. If this happens, consult the vet who may administer hormones to burst the cyst or may, with a bad case, suggest a hysterectomy.

False pregnancy (pseudopregnancy)
The more common form of false pregnancy begins to eight or nine weeks after a heat, and may last quite a few weeks. Signs include: ☐ increased appetite ☐ odd behaviour – nursing toys and slippers ☐ straining ☐ breast enlargement ☐ sluggishness ☐ displays of affection ☐ abdominal swelling ☐ lactation.

This problem can recur after each heat. There are various ways of solving it, including drugs or spaying.

Breast tumour
An unspayed bitch may show cyclical changes in the breasts which can lead to tumours. If you notice any lumps or swellings in your bitch's breasts, consult the vet with a view to having them removed. Not all breast tumours are malignant but you should check the breasts by feeling them at least every two months, particularly following a heat. Benign lumps are often clearer in outline than malignancies.

Metritis
This is a womb infection which may occur within a couple of weeks of whelping. Signs include: ☐ purulent, yellow/green discharge ☐ dullness ☐ lack of appetite ☐ vomiting. Treatment involves prompt veterinary prescription of antibiotics or spaying.

SPECIAL BREED PROBLEMS

Boxer, Chihuahua – prone to cryptorchidism
Chow Chow – prone to inertia during whelping and difficulty in mating
Bulldog, Pug (and other flat-nosed breeds), – prone to difficulty in whelping

Heart, blood and circulation disorders

The dog has a four-chamber mammalian heart. Two atria empty blood into the ventricles which drive the blood around. The right ventricle pumps blood to the lungs to eliminate carbon dioxide and to pick up oxygen. This blood returns to the left atrium, which empties it into the left ventricle to be pumped round the body. Many heart diseases in dogs are caused by congenital deformities. There is a variety of anatomical malformations of varing severity which may involve holes in the heart, transposed blood vessels or connections between vessels.

The general signs of heart disease are:
☐ tiredness ☐ poor ability to exercise ☐ coughing after a period of lying down (a "cardiac cough") ☐ "blueness" of the gums ☐ fainting.

> **SEE ALSO:**
> **Taking a dog's pulse** see p.42.

Patent ductus
A congenital condition may occur where a foetal blood vessel which should be sealed, remains open. This vessel then acts as a shunt between the two sides of the circulatory system (which should not normally be connected). Similar congenital deformities of the vessels around the heart may form a ring which traps the oesophagus, preventing the passage of solids and causing vomiting (see *Vascular rings* p.53). Surgical correction of this type of deformity is often successful.

Heart "murmur"
Inside the heart, between the *atria* and the *ventricles* (see diagram, right) are valves which prevent blood flowing back into the atria when the ventricles contract to pump blood out. Sometimes, due to congenital deformities or age changes in the valves, they may not close efficiently, allowing some leakage back into the atria under pressure. The sound that this blood makes as it squirts back into the atria can be heard through a stethoscope and is therefore called a "murmur".

Murmur on left side of heart
Small breeds in particular seem susceptible to this problem as they get older. A weakness in the *mitral valve* on the left side of the heart causes a rise in pressure in the blood returning from the lungs, forcing small amounts of fluid out into the lung. This hinders the exchange of oxygen for carbon dioxide. Signs are ☐ reduced exercise ability ☐ "cardiac cough" (especially when the dog wakes after resting) due to fluid accumulated in the lungs.

Murmur on right side of heart
Similar problems occur when the murmur is due to a failure of the *tricuspid valve* on the right side of the heart. In this case, the fluid collects in the abdomen, producing dropsy (swollen abdomen) and an enlarged liver and spleen. The signs are the same as for a left-side murmur, but with swelling of the abdomen.

What is the treatment for heart conditions?
There are no suitable home remedies for heart conditions in dogs, but it is sensible to watch for and avoid obesity (see p.61), which places undue strain on the heart.

If you're worried about your dog's exercise tolerance, or you suspect a cardiac cough, seek veterinary help. Your vet can control these symptoms with drugs and early treatment reduces the chance of complications.

Sophisticated techniques are available for treatment of heart conditions. Your vet may initially examine your dog with a stethoscope, but may well carry out an E.C.G. examination to detect abnormal rhythms in the heart. These are treated with drugs used for the same conditions in humans. Surgery may be a possibility for some of the less complex congenital abnormalities, especially vascular rings (see p.53) and patent ductus (see p.74).

New heart valves, as used in humans, aren't fitted to dogs. Treatment is by medical methods, primarily with drugs called "diuretics". By making the dog pass more urine, these move fluid along as it accumulates. Drugs may also be used to strengthen the dog's heartbeat.

Heartworms
Dogs' may be infested by internal parasites called "heartworms" which live in blood vessels. *Angiostrongylus*, the heartworm, is transmitted via slugs eaten by the dog. Its larvae leave blood vessels in the lung, are coughed up and passed in the faeces.
What is the treatment?
Ridding the dog's body of heartworms is fairly difficult due to the danger of dead adult worms in the blood system causing a thrombosis. Treatment must be carried out in the vet's surgery, usually after supportive care to get the dog in the best possible health before giving drugs to kill the worms.

Anaemia
A condition due to a reduced number of red blood cells and/or a reduction in the amount of *haemoglobin* (red pigment in the blood which carries oxygen). The three major causes of anaemia are:
1 Destruction of red blood cells by:
□ parasites □ poisons □ bacterial toxins □ immune reactions.
2 Loss of blood as a result of:
□ accidents □ poisoning □ bleeding ulcers □ parasites (such as hookworms or whipworms).
3 Reduced or abnormal production of new red blood cells in the bone marrow, due to: □ tumours □ poisons □ acute infections □ chronic septic conditions (such as pyometra or purulent wounds) □ chronic kidney disease (see p.70) □ mineral deficiencies (iron, copper or cobalt) □ vitamin deficiencies (Vitamins B_6 or B_{12}).

The signs of anaemia include: □ pallor in the mouth and round the eyes (loss of normal pink colour) □ gradual weakness □ inability to exercise □ rapid breathing □ being unsettled.
What is the treatment?
If you think your dog is anaemic, consult the vet who will take blood samples to assess the degree, type and cause of the anaemia. Your vet will treat the underlying cause as appropriate and may give your dog anti-anaemic drugs such as iron supplements, vitamins and anabolic steroids. Very severe cases may need a blood transfusion. Once your vet has diagnosed anaemia, you'll be instructed to feed your dog highly nutritious foods, good quality protein, vitamin supplements and liver. Don't overtire your dog during its convalescence.

SPECIAL BREED PROBLEMS
King Charles Spaniel, Pekingese, Poodle – prone to heart murmur
Greyhound – prone to heartworms (due to being kept in kennels in large numbers)

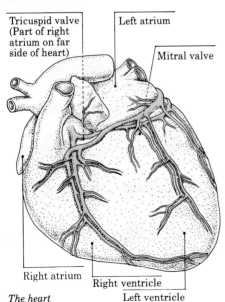

Tricuspid valve (Part of right atrium on far side of heart)

Left atrium

Mitral valve

Right atrium

Right ventricle

Left ventricle

The heart

Neurological disorders

Many problems can afflict the dog's nervous system. The nerves, the brain or the spine may all be affected. Damage to the membranes surrounding the brain and the spinal cord results in *meningitis*; damage to the brain is the problem with *encephalitis*. Both conditions are caused by bacterial infections. Signs of brain damage include: □ fits □ twitching □ tremors □ nystagmus (sideways flicking of the eyes.

SEE ALSO:

Muscle, bone and joint disorders see pp.78–9.
Convulsions see p.90.

Epilepsy

This is quite common, especially in dogs of between one and three years old. It may be caused by:

● Inherited epilepsy
● Previous injury or oxygen starvation to the brain
● Hydrocephalus (see right)
● Distemper (see opposite)
● Tumours.

Some dogs suffer frequent fits, others more occasional ones. There's no set pattern so if two occur close together, it doesn't necessarily mean they're getting worse. However, fits may worsen as a dog gets older, due to the effect of other diseases.

What are the signs?
Strangely enough, fits occur when a dog is relaxed and quiet. They are usually short (about five minutes) and include a period of unconsciousness. For physical signs of a fit, see p.90.

What is the treatment?
For the immediate course of action, see *First Aid* p.90. Long-term treatment means veterinary prescribed anticonvulsants. These may not totally abolish the fits but should reduce their frequency. Dogs having a sequence of continual fits lasting 15–30 minutes should be reported to the vet urgently; intravenous anticonvulsants may be needed.

Hydrocephalus

Literally "water on the brain", this usually occurs through a deformity in the drainage system from the fluid-filled ventricles of the brain. Eventually, the brain tissues are compressed against the skull, and various signs occur which may include: □ fits □ blindness □ incoordination □ dullness.

Successful treatment involves early diagnosis and specialist surgery.

Encephalitis

This means an inflammation of the brain. It may occur due to bacterial infections, viruses like distemper or even old age. Infectious causes are usually very sudden. Bacterial encephalitis often follows ear disease, wounds or skull fractures. Signs include: □ fits □ head pressing □ stiff neck □ painful head.

Whatever the reason for its onset, encephalitis needs prompt veterinary treatment since the various causes require different drugs.

Strokes

It isn't certain whether dogs truly suffer strokes like people, but they certainly show similar signs, including: □ sudden collapse □ interference with the function of various parts of the body □ walking in circles □ droopy eyelids □ partial paralysis □ eye flicking.

Consult a vet immediately if your dog shows these signs. Steroids can reduce the symptoms; other drugs can improve the blood flow in the brain. Treatment is often quite successful for a time.

Distemper (hardpad)

This condition occurs most often in young dogs between three and six months old, but can attack at any age.

Infection occurs through inhalation of the virus and is spread around the body by defensive cells trying to capture and kill it. If they fail, the virus attacks the immune and nervous systems and the cells lining the lungs and gut.

What are the signs?

A young, fit dog picking up a very light infection may fight it successfully, showing dullness and a slight temperature. Full-blown cases show a high temperature then a second stage:
□ dullness □ nasal and eye discharge coughing □ vomiting □ diarrhoea □ thickening and cracking of the skin of the nose and pads.

The nervous signs

As the second phase symptoms are improving, about four weeks after initial infection, the nervous system may start to show damage. This can range from slight tremors to full epileptic fits.

What is the treatment?

Antibiotics, cough suppressants and drugs to treat vomiting and diarrhoea are usually required, possibly plus anticonvulsants for dogs with nervous damage.

The real answer to distemper is vaccination (see p.49). Dogs particularly at risk can be given antiserum – very short-term protection which shouldn't be confused with proper vaccination.

Cervical spondylopathy

This disease, whose sufferers are known as "wobblers", tends to affect larger breeds. One (or more) cervical vertebrae are malformed and this, combined with the weight of the dog's head, bruises the spinal cord. Signs include: □ trailing the forefeet □ scuffing and wearing down nails □ wobbling gait □ unsteady hindquarters (especially after exercise) □ paralysis (partial or total).

What is the treatment?

Take your dog to the vet who will X-ray its neck. Surgical treatment may be possible if the problem is detected early enough. But once paralysis sets in, the future is generally grim.

Slipped disc

More correctly called "disc protrusion", this is a common disorder in short-legged, long-backed breeds. These dogs' discs age more rapidly than in other breeds; the centre of a disc may push through the soft outer layers, damaging nerves in the spinal cord. The signs are:
□ sudden pain □ unwillingness to move □ limping □ hunched posture □ inability to raise the head □ paralysis (partial or total).

What is the treatment?

If your dog is in sudden pain accompanied by the other signs, don't delay – consult a vet immediately. Cases showing milder pain or a limp may respond to treatment with drugs, but surgery is indicated for worse cases.

Rabies

This killer viral disease is transmitted by saliva from an infected dog.
Signs include: □ inability to swallow □ furious running, biting □ drowsiness □ paralysis. The virus moves back down the nerves to the salivary glands where it multiplies. Affected animals will die; humans in contact with them are in danger and must be vaccinated immediately.

In countries where rabies is present, vaccination will protect your dog. Keep it under constant supervision. If bitten by a suspect dog, you must immediately:
● Clean the wound with soap or disinfectant.
● Seek medical attention.
● Safely restrain the dog if possible.
● If this is impossible, call the police.

SPECIAL BREED PROBLEMS

Basset –prone to slipped disc, cervical spondylopathy
Chihuahua, King Charles Spaniel, poodles –prone to hydrocephalus
Dachshund, Pekingese, Shih Tzu – prone to slipped disc
Great Dane, Dobermann – prone to cervical spondylopathy

Muscle, bone and joint disorders

The skeleton is a system of bony levers moved by muscles which are anchored at crucial points on the bones. The bones are linked together at joints which act like shock absorbers. Although body shape and skeleton are very diverse, dogs' muscles vary little between breeds. Diseases of the muscles, bones or joints are relatively common in dogs – injuries resulting from falls, fights or road accidents being some of the most usual causes. Minor injuries such as sprains may be treatable at home, but if your dog is in pain, contact the vet. Signs are: □ limping □ pain □ swelling.

SEE ALSO:

Nutritional diseases see p.61.
Splints and bandages see p.93.
Slipped disc, cervical spondylopathy see p.77.

Muscular problems

A muscle disease is called a "myopathy"; inflamed muscle is known as "myositis". There are various causes of myopathy, including bacterial infections. Some are inherited and breed-specific. They have no treatment. Others *do* have specific treatments; consult the vet immediately if you suspect them.

What is the treatment for myopathy?
If you suspect that your dog has mild muscle damage (a slight limp which disappears within 24 hours), try two days' rest. If this relieves it, continue the rest treatment for a while. But if in any doubt, consult the vet.

Eosinophilic myositis
The cause of this disease is unknown. It affects the muscles of the head, causing pain and, later, wasting of the muscles. Signs include: □ weakness □ stiffness □ pain □ lop-sided look to the head.

Eosinophilic myositis needs urgent veterinary help. Your vet can prescribe anti-inflammatory drugs and pain killers.

Joint problems

Arthritis (inflammation of the joints) is fairly common in dogs. The major causes are anatomical abnormalities which may either be hereditary or have nutritional causes (see p.61).

Sprains and osteoarthritis
A sprain is damage to a joint, which may mean torn ligaments or fractured cartilage. This also causes arthritis which, if severe or untreated, can result in osteoarthritis – inflammation of the bone in the joint. Once osteoarthritis sets in, the damage is usually permanent.

LIMPING

The major sign of a limb disorder is a limp. Try to assess the severity of the injury by checking the following:

Things to look for
● Dog carrying its leg clear of the ground or just dabbing it down
● Painful swelling. Both these signs suggest a fairly serious injury

● Dog "favouring" one leg, even if there's no pain or swelling

Possible causes
● Sprain (see above)
● Fracture
● Wound or other injury (see p.92)

Treatment
However slight the damage, rest your dog until the condition has improved and in most cases, for a week after this. If a few days' rest doesn't cure an apparently minor limp, seek veterinary advice.

Urgency
✚✚ If there's pain or the limp persists, consult the vet as soon as convenient.

What is the treatment?
For first aid, see *Treating a sprain* p.93. Serious sprains should be rested for about six weeks, after which you should slowly re-introduce exercise. You may find support bandages useful.

Osteoarthritis has no cure so all efforts should be aimed at alleviating it. Strict rest is the most important treatment you can give and veterinary drugs can reduce the inflammation.

Warning: Pain killers may enable a dog to use an injured joint which could result in permanent damage. If your vet prescribes pain killers, you must also rest the dog.

Bone diseases

Certain diseases of dog's bones are congenital, but others are due to some disruption in the body's provision of nutrients and oxygen. A fairly common problem, known as *osteochondritis dissecans*, is seen especially in large breeds. Due to inadequate nutrition, an area of shoulder cartilage dies and falls into the joint, where it sometimes revives and grows to form a loose lump called a "joint mouse". This rubs on the joint, causing arthritis.

Over-rapid growth is probably involved in the development of this disease. The elbow, knee and hock bones can also be affected. Signs include: □ lameness □ swelling □ pain □ local heat.

Fortunately, prompt surgery to remove the joint mouse usually results in almost complete recovery.

Fractures

A fracture can occur in almost any bone in the dog's body. Spontaneous fractures can occur in conditions like *osteoporosis* where the bones are thin. Signs include: □ acute lameness □ swelling □ pain □ local heat.

What is the treatment?
Don't delay – consult a vet immediately or there may be severe malformation or failure to heal. (For procedure after an accident, see p.88.)

Hip dysplasia

This disease is quite common. Malformation of the hip joint means the ball and socket connection fits badly. The head of the femur rubs on the edges of the joint, causing arthritis.

The problem is most common among large breeds. There's a strong inherited component, so many breed societies and veterinary authorities have set up certification schemes based on X-rays. Find out if there's a scheme for your breed before buying a puppy and ask to see its parents' certificates (issued at one year of age).

What is the treatment?
Pain killers may alleviate the problem in young, growing dogs. Restrict exercise severely for up to six months, after which you can gradually build up to a normal lifestyle. However, more serious cases will require surgery.

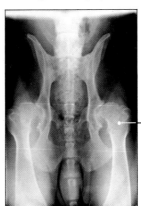

Malformed hip joint

X-ray showing hip dysplasia

SPECIAL BREED PROBLEMS

German Shepherd – prone to eosinophilic myositis, osteochondritis dissecans in elbow, hip dysplasia
Rottweiler, St. Bernard – prone to osteochondritis dissecans
Labrador – prone to osteochondritis dissecans in elbow, hip dysplasia

Skin and coat disorders

The dog's skin and coat are inextricably linked. The coat is made up of a mass of hairs, each of which grows from a follicle in the inner layer of the skin. Skin diseases in dogs can be complex. A common diagnosis is *eczema* – a general term for inflamed skin – but identifying the actual cause is often difficult.

The basic sequence of a skin disease is inflammation (dermatitis), causing irritation (itching) which makes the dog scratch with its claws or teeth. This results in loss of hair, more inflammation and more itching – the "itch-scratch-itch cycle". Finally, bacteria invade the broken skin. The most important part of treatment is preventing the dog from scratching; this may call for anti-inflammatory drugs and sedatives.

What are the signs of skin disease?
Major signs of skin disease include:
□ scratching □ hair loss □ reddened skin □ areas wet from licking (often stained brown by saliva in white dogs) □ rashes □ infected spots □ black, gritty material in the coat □ insects in the coat □ mats □ dry coat □ dandruff.

> ### SEE ALSO:
> **Parasites** see p.62.
> **Mats and tangles** see p.29.
> **Moulting** see p.24.

Mites
Three types of mite can cause problems in dogs:
● Demodex – causes demodectic mange
● Sarcoptes – causes sarcoptic mange
● Otodectes – causes inflammation of the ear

Otodectes is the only type of mite visible to the naked eye and then only rarely; you may see them as tiny white moving dots in the ear.
Demodex
Carried by most dogs, this mite usually causes no trouble, but it may be a nuisance at times of stress and in young animals whose natural defences aren't fully developed. Demodex causes a type of pustular dermatitis in puppies, around the head and shoulders. This often becomes infected – a condition known as "juvenile pyoderma". Signs include:
□ characteristic "mousy" odour □ hair loss □ flaky, oily skin.
What is the treatment?
Unless dogs receive veterinary attention within 24 hours of this developing, very serious scarring can occur. Your vet can prescribe drugs and antibiotics which give effective relief. Special shampoos can control the oiliness of the coat and the characteristic smell.
Sarcoptic mange (Scabies)
More commonly known as "scabies", this problem can affect humans as well as dogs of any age. The sarcoptes burrow through the skin, producing tunnels in which they lay eggs. Although the infection usually dies away in humans, it should still be treated. The sign of this in the dog is an itchy rash of red spots, especially on ears, elbows and hocks. On human skin the "tunnels" can actually be seen.
What is the treatment?
Prompt treatment is important, to avoid human infection and to prevent the dog damaging itself seriously by scratching and biting. The vet will prescribe special chemicals to be applied in insecticidal shampoos every five days for at least four weeks (the eggs take up to three weeks to hatch). The vet may also prescribe drugs to help stop self-mutilation by biting and scratching.

> ### SPECIAL BREED PROBLEMS
> *Dobermann* – prone to demodex and juvenile pyoderma
> *Dachschund* – prone to juvenile pyoderma
> *Irish Setter* – prone to demodex

SCRATCHING

This common sign of skin disease has many possible causes.

Things to look for
- Parasites (fleas, lice and mites, see p.62)
- Bacterial sores – small, infected spots and scaly, red inflamed areas

Possible causes
- Parasite infestation
- Ear disease (see p.64)
- Impacted anal sacs (indicated by dog licking sores at base of tail, see p.60)
- Contact dermatitis (indicated by redness on the belly)

Treatment
Aim to treat the specific cause.
- If indicated, use an antiparasitic bath (if in doubt treat for fleas).
- Wash localized bacterial sores with antibacterial wash.
- Generalized bacterial sores, ear problems or impacted anal sacs need veterinary attention.
- With contact dermatitis, cut off access to likely causes such as nylon carpet, car seat covers, disinfectant on floors. If home treatment fails, consult a vet.

Urgency
✚✚ If the skin is broken and "sticky" or chewed, consult a vet as soon as convenient.

REDDENED SKIN

You may notice this sign before the skin problem becomes fully established.

Possible causes
- Fleas (see p.62)
- Contact dermatitis
- Allergic dermatitis
- Anything causing itching – ringworm, lice or bacterial sores

Treatment
- If the reddened area is very localized, apply calamine lotion.
- If the problem is more generalized, a lanolin baby shampoo will wash out potential irritants and cool the skin. When the dog is dry, apply flea spray. If the problem is still evident after 24 hours, consult the vet.

Urgency
✚✚ Consult a vet as soon as convenient.

HAIR LOSS

There are a variety of factors involved in hair loss in dogs.

Things to look for
- Broken hairs in coat
- Inflamed, red skin
- Bald areas
- Symmetrical hair loss
- Excessive, prolonged moult

Possible causes
- Scratching (indicated by reddening of skin and broken hairs)
- Malfunction in the hair growth cycle indicated by bald areas with no irritation
- Diet

Treatment
To treat scratching, see above. The most common causes of hair loss without irritation are hormonal and need veterinary treatment.
If diet is the problem, multivitamins and extra oil may stop the moult. If there's no response after a few weeks, consult the vet.

Urgency
✚ Dietary problems may be treatable at home.
✚✚ Otherwise, consult a vet as soon as convenient.

Veterinary care and nursing

It is a good idea to choose a vet that has been recommended by friends or the breeder of your puppy. Before registering with a vet, find out:
● What are the consulting hours?
● Is there an appointments system or not?
● How early must you phone for a routine appointment?
● Does the practice make house calls?
● What are the arrangements for emergency night calls?
● Are records kept so that your dog's medical history can be sent on to a new vet if you move?

Taking your dog to the surgery
Whenever possible, telephone the surgery to make an appointment if this is the system they use. Withhold food and water from your dog before you visit the vet in case it needs an operation.

Check first to see if the surgery has a separate cat and puppy waiting room. If it has, this is the place for unvaccinated, healthy puppies. Once you have checked in, keep your dog under control on a short lead. Many dogs are tense at the vet's and fights occur easily. Small dogs are often best held on your lap, whilst very sick dogs are often best kept in the car until just before you are called. This avoids exposing other animals to infectious diseases.

The consulting room
Don't let your dog loose as you enter the consulting room; hang on to the lead and keep it under control. Most vets like to let the dog relax first, and will ask you various questions whilst it settles.

Be prepared to tell your vet:
● Your dog's breed, sex and age
● How long you have had the dog
● Its recent history and whether it has recently spent time in kennels
● Whether it has recently encountered any disease
● When it was last vaccinated
● Why you have called and what signs of illness you have observed
● If your dog is eating, drinking and passing urine and faeces normally.

RESTRAINING A DOG

The degree of restraint needed during examination and treatment varies according to the dog and the procedure to be carried out. However, it is usual for the dog to be placed on a table. Hold the dog yourself; it is less likely to cause problems. If you feel it may bite, use a tape muzzle (see p.89). It helps if your dog is used to being held.
To restrain a small dog Grasp the scruff tightly including the collar. Don't try to grab the nose – you risk being bitten.
To restrain a medium-sized dog (see right) Tuck the head under your upper arm, place the other arm around the body and grasp one of its forelegs.
To restrain a large dog Place one arm under the neck and fix the head with your other hand by grasping the outer foreleg and leaning your body over its shoulders. Someone else should hold the rear end.

Restraining a medium-sized dog

THE VET'S EXAMINATION

Unless the problem is obviously localized, the vet will examine your dog's whole body, starting at the head and working downwards.

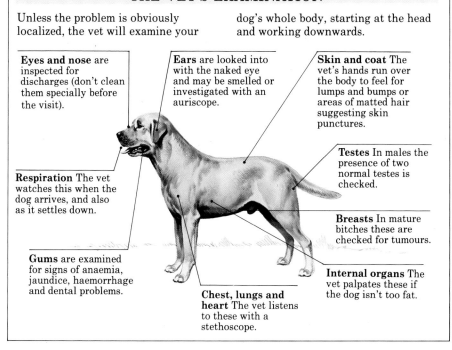

Eyes and nose are inspected for discharges (don't clean them specially before the visit).

Ears are looked into with the naked eye and may be smelled or investigated with an auriscope.

Skin and coat The vet's hands run over the body to feel for lumps and bumps or areas of matted hair suggesting skin punctures.

Respiration The vet watches this when the dog arrives, and also as it settles down.

Testes In males the presence of two normal testes is checked.

Breasts In mature bitches these are checked for tumours.

Gums are examined for signs of anaemia, jaundice, haemorrhage and dental problems.

Chest, lungs and heart The vet listens to these with a stethoscope.

Internal organs The vet palpates these if the dog isn't too fat.

Operations

Procedures do vary from vet to vet, but generally you'll be asked to starve your dog from 6pm the previous evening and give it no fluids after bedtime. On arrival at the surgery, the dog will be admitted by a nurse and you'll be requested to sign a "consent form" permitting the surgery or necessary treatment. The nurse may give your dog a mild pre-operative sedative to minimize the amount of anaesthetic needed.

Most initial anaesthetics are injected. A tube is then inserted into the trachea through which gaseous anaesthetic is passed to keep the dog asleep during the operation. Recovery begins when the gas is turned off and the dog breathes air. This takes about an hour and at this point, the dog is just able to stand. After a minor operation, you'll probably be allowed to collect your pet the same day.

Euthanasia

Unfortunately, your dog may eventually need to be "put to sleep", on the advice of the vet. Your vet can arrange for this to happen at the surgery or in your home; you can ask to be present if you wish. If you have a dog euthanized at home, it is likely the vet will need your help.

The standard method of euthanasia is the injection of a large overdose of an anaesthetic drug. This is usually injected into the foreleg. The brain will often be asleep and the heart stopped before the injection is complete. Euthanasia is peaceful and painless. All the dog feels is a slight prick in its foreleg.

Some owners like to bury their dogs at home, but if this is impractical, all vets have access to cremation services who will individually cremate dogs and return their ashes if you wish.

Home nursing

A sick dog needs gentle care and nursing. Once your vet has diagnosed the illness and prescribed appropriate medication, you'll probably be allowed to take it home where it can convalesce and recover. Your main responsibilities are:
● Providing a warm, hygienic rest area
● Feeding a tempting, nutritious diet
● Giving medicines prescribed by the vet
● Checking dressings or wounds as directed by the vet.

Change your dog's bedding frequently. When the dog needs to go out, just give it enough time to pass urine and faeces before making it come back indoors.

Keeping the dog warm
Make sure your dog is kept warm and out of draughts. Supplement household heating with carefully positioned infra-red or dull-emitting bulbs, placed at least 60 cm away from the dog (test heat with your hand on the dog). Well-wrapped hot-water bottles are useful too – remember to refill them regularly.

Feeding a sick dog
Loss of appetite is a common sign of illness in animals. But it is important that your dog eats: it needs nourishment to help it recover.

Sit on the floor beside your dog. Offer it spoonfuls of food or liquid while you talk to it encouragingly. If this fails, spoonfeed as described below.

Nourishing liquid feeds like broth or meat stock help keep up the dog's spirits and maintain its strength. Your vet may instruct you to add glucose or special sachets of power or liquid to the dog's drinking water. Starvation is unlikely but dehydration is a real possibility, particularly in a dog which has had diarrhoea or vomiting. *Make sure your*

SPOONFEEDING A DOG

If the food is pleasant-tasting and your dog placid, you'll probably be able to spoonfeed it on your own. But generally this is a two-person job.
Safety first: After each spoonful, let the dog's mouth open a little to allow it to swallow. Be extra careful with short-nosed breeds like Pugs Pekingese and Bulldogs; these may bite or have trouble breathing; their soft palate can constrict the pharynx.

1 The helper kneels by the dog's left side and raises its head by placing his or her right arm round the dog's neck and across the front. With the left hand, the helper should gently hold its nose.

2 The feeder can now spoon food into the right-hand side of the dog's mouth or pour liquids into the "pouch" formed by the side of the lower lip. For more substantial foods, the helper can relax the grip.

dog drinks water. If coaxing fails, give water in a spoon (see below left).

Invalid foods

Unless the vet advises a special diet, feed your dog a variety of tempting, nutritious, tissue-building foods. Choose easily digested foods rich in protein, minerals and vitamins such as:

Liquids

☐ glucose (two teaspoons per teacupful of water) ☐ honey ☐ beef tea ☐ calf's foot jelly (warmed) ☐ proprietary liquid foods.

Solids

☐ white fish ☐ best-quality mince ☐ cheese ☐ cooked eggs ☐ meat- and fish-based baby foods ☐ mashed potatoes ☐ cooked rice ☐ baby cereals.

Giving medicines

Give liquid medicines by spoonfeeding (see below left), but remember few medicines are pleasant-tasting and you may encounter some resistance.

Giving tablets

If your vet prescribes tablets, don't crush them – the centres often taste very bitter. You'll probably need a helper unless the dog is very ill or very placid. As with spoonfeeding, a second person should hold the dog – one arm round the neck to lift its head and one steadying the hindquarters.

The other person should grip the dog's upper jaw firmly with one hand, tucking the skin of the muzzle around and into the mouth with finger and thumb. The other hand containing the tablet is used to push the lower jaw downwards and propel the tablet to the back of the tongue. (If necessary, give it a push with your finger or a blunt instrument.)

If your dog won't swallow tablets given like this, try placing the tablet in the mouth, giving a spoonful of water and closing the mouth to make it swallow. Some dogs will only eat tablets smeared with butter or cheese.

MAKING AN ELIZABETHAN COLLAR

A useful device which you can construct from a plastic bucket – 4.5 litre size for small dogs, 9 litre for larger dogs – this collar prevents a convalescent dog from scratching its head or ears, pawing a head or eye wound, or turning to lick or chew at its hindquarters.

1 With a heated knife, remove the base of the bucket. Make holes round the bottom, 5 cm apart and 5 cm from the edge.

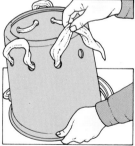

2 Thread a 5 cm bandage through the holes, leaving a loop between each pair, large enough to fit the dog's collar.

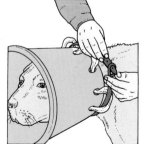

3 Insert the collar through the loops. Place the bucket over the dog's head and fasten the collar comfortably.

Care of the elderly dog

The number of years of a dog's life varies considerably between breeds. In general, the small (not toy) breeds live longer. However, the two chief signs of old age are common to most dogs – greying of hair round the head (especially near the ears and muzzle) and loss of weight.

Elderly dogs lose weight mainly because of a failing liver and kidneys – these problems are accompanied by increased thirst and a good appetite. Once you notice weight loss in your elderly dog, it is worth taking it to the vet for three- to six-monthly checks. Often, a timely course of anabolic steroids will slow down the physical deterioration. Sometimes, these problems are caused by minor attacks of leptospirosis (see pp.56 and 71). If your dog has been vaccinated routinely throughout its life, it may avoid suffering in this way.

Although chronic kidney failure (see p.70) isn't painful, it often culminates in acute kidney failure. If you see any of the signs of acute kidney or liver failure (see pp.70 and 55), consult your vet.

FEEDING TIPS FOR ELDERLY DOGS

A good home-cooked diet for "geriatrics" is given on p.37.
- Make sure you're giving the dog enough food if its appetite is good
- Give easily-digested foods like fish and poultry
- Don't forget the importance of extra vitamins (see p.37)
- Keep drinking water available at all times
- Use bran and/or liquid paraffin to combat constipation
- Add fat (lard, chicken or turkey fat) to the diet to provide extra calories for lean, elderly dogs – one teaspoon for small dogs, four for larger breeds

---

Bowel and bladder problems

Some old dogs become quite constipated – often due to prostate problems (see p.72). Others may lose some degree of control over their bladder; this may be due to cystitis (see p.71). Tumours in the anus may interfere with its function, causing loss of control of the bowel. If any of these problems becomes frequent, consult your vet. They may be painful, or upset a habitually clean dog. There's no need for you to suffer these conditions in silence – all can be treated with some measure of success.

Caring for the teeth

If you're in any doubt about the health of your dog's teeth, mention this to your vet on one of the routine visits. Brushing the teeth and giving material for chewing during a dog's younger years (see p.54) minimizes the build-up of tartar. Elderly dogs may not chew bones any longer, so it is worthwhile brushing the teeth once or twice a week (see p.54). Despite this, tartar is still liable to build up and may need removing under anaesthetic.

Eye and ear problems

Although an old dog's eyesight and hearing often become impaired, its slower lifestyle may compensate for this. Handle your dog gently, taking care not to startle it with sudden loud noises – make sure your dog can see you before you switch on any household appliances such as the vacuum cleaner. Check behind your car before reversing outside your home. For coping with a blind dog, see p.68.

Bone and joint problems

Elderly dogs are often bothered by general stiffness associated with arthritis in some of their joints. This is more of a problem in overweight dogs or large breeds. Ask your vet's advice; he or she may prescribe pain killers which can considerably ease a dog's life.

Keeping your dog healthy

With sensible care, you can considerably reduce the likelihood of your pet succumbing to illness. Responsible ownership means considering its needs always. For a healthy dog:

● Follow the advice on choosing a healthy puppy (see p.11).

● Be aware of any diseases or conditions to which your puppy's breed is prone. Obtain relevant clearance certificates where available and keep a lookout for signs of the problems throughout the dog's life.

● Have your puppy properly vaccinated (see p.49) and keep up to date with annual boosters. For these routine annual visits, prepare a list of any problems or questions you may have for the vet.

● Don't try to boost your dog's growth rate too much through the puppy stage – rapid growth can give rise to muscle and bone problems.

● Establish a routine for checking your dog's skin, eyes and ears at grooming sessions. This gives you more chance of spotting any problems early.

● Avoid obesity in your dog (see p.61).

● Keep your dog's bedding and feeding utensils scrupulously clean – hygiene is a crucial factor in good health.

● Keep your dog clean too – check its eyes, ears, nose, mouth, skin, genital and anal areas regularly to ensure they're free of discharges.

Safety precautions

Never let your dog off your property alone. Roaming dogs can be involved in, or even cause, a road accident. Roamers are much more likely to get into fights, upsetting other dog-owners, and may also chase sheep.

Take your dog for walks regularly, even if you have a large garden. A routine walk gives you the opportunity to reinforce basic training lessons (see pp.20–3); always keep your dog under control when it is out with you.

A healthy dog at the prime of life
A fit dog, full of stamina, is the reward of proper feeding, grooming and exercise.

Are you insured?

It is well worth taking out veterinary insurance, particularly for urban dogs whose risk of being involved in fights or road accidents is high. Modern veterinary treatment has paralleled human medical techniques in many of its newer advances, but these can carry high costs. A modest annual premium can ease the burden of unexpected illness and accidents.

ZOONOSES

There are a few canine diseases which also affect humans. These are known as "zoonoses", and the most important are:

● Rabies (see p.75)

● Ringworm (see p.62)

● Fleas (see p.62)

● Roundworm (see p.63)

Simple precautions can help avoid all these. Regular worming, use of flea sprays during the summer months and washing your hands after handling a dog with any kind of skin problems, are normal measures to take. If you should ever be bitten by a "suspect" dog in a rabies area, seek medical advice immediately.

Accidents and emergencies

One of the most upsetting things that can happen to your dog is a car accident. Dealing with a dog at the site of an accident can be a job for the vet – a dog may need extricating from the underside of a car, or may have become too dangerous (through pain or fear) to be handled by inexperienced people.

In general, though, it is best not to waste time waiting for the vet to arrive. Few vets are equipped with more than a visiting bag out of hours and all specialized equipment is at the surgery. Phone ahead to warn the vet of your arrival and take the dog to the surgery. If the vet is away, he or she can advise the staff what to do in the meantime.

ACCIDENT PROCEDURE

1 Don't panic. Approach the dog cautiously and speak reassuringly (the best person to do this is the owner).
2 Gently restrain the dog with a "lead" made from a belt or piece of rope. Form a noose and drop it over the dog's head.
3 Improvise a muzzle (see opposite).
4 Ensure the dog isn't trapped.
5 Apply necessary first aid. Look for:
● Heartbeat (on left side of chest)
● Breathing movement
● Major haemorrhage
● Gasping
● Pale gums
● Inability to stand
● Obvious fractures
6 Telephone the vet's surgery, stating which of these signs are present.
7 Move the dog carefully (see p.90)

SEE ALSO:

Collapse see p.90.
Control of bleeding see p.92.
Bandaging see p.93.
Shock see opposite.

A BASIC FIRST AID KIT

Although many of your own first aid items are suitable for dogs, it is preferable to keep a separate kit.

1 Round-ended scissors 2 Stubby-bulb thermometer (not the family's)
3 Tweezers 4 5 cm and 10 cm bandages
5 5 cm adhesive tape dressing 6 Lint gauze 7 Cotton wool 8 Old socks
9 Plastic bags for keeping foot dressings dry 10 Antiseptic cream
11 Antiseptic wash 12 Cotton buds
13 Kaolin tablets or medicine
14 Calamine lotion 15 Proprietary eye wash 16 Proprietary ear cleaner
17 Medicinal liquid paraffin.

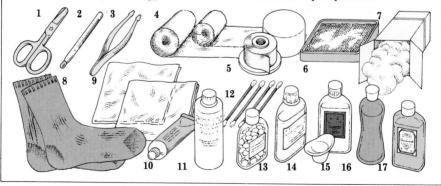

IMPROVISING A MUZZLE

A frightened dog in pain may try to bite, so an improvised muzzle is a sensible precaution. Use a bandage, or a necktie (belts are too stiff).

Watch for the dog going blue or having trouble breathing. If this happens, untie the muzzle, open the mouth and pull the tongue forward. Then keep the muzzle loose and hold the dog's head on your lap.

● **Never** muzzle a dog with chest injuries or one having trouble breathing

● **Never** leave a muzzled dog alone – it may try to remove the muzzle

● **Never** muzzle a short-nosed breed – you may impair its breathing

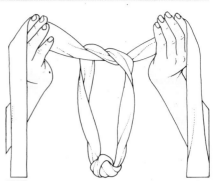

1 Tie a tight knot in the centre of the bandage or tie, so that it "hangs". Make a second, loose knot, about 20 cm above the first.

2 Slip the loop formed between the knots well back over the nose. Pull the second knot tight, so the first catches under the jaw.

3 Bring the two ends down on either side; cross them under the jaw. Take them round and tie at the back in an easily loosened double bow.

SHOCK AND COLLAPSE

If your dog has collapsed, quick action on your part may mean the difference between life and death. For the correct action to take, see p.90. If conscious, it may be suffering from shock. Possible causes of collapse include: ☐ epileptic fit (see p.76) ☐ acute infection ☐ heart disease (see p.74) ☐ poisoning (see p.91) ☐ diabetes (see p.57) ☐ exposure ☐ heatstroke (see p.91) ☐ accident injury (see p.88) ☐ haemorrhage.

DO NOT:

● Give alcoholic stimulants
● Move the dog more than necessary
● Raise the dog's head or prop it up
● Give the dog anything by mouth

SEE ALSO:

Pulse see p.42.
Restraint see p.82.
Convulsions see p.90.

MOVING AN INJURED DOG

Move an injured dog as gently as you can. Transfer the dog to a blanket which can be used as a stretcher. Ideally three people are needed – to support the head, back and pelvis. (If help isn't available, carefully move the dog on to the blanket one section at a time.)

1 If necessary, use a muzzle and lead. Spread the blanket behind the dog and move it gently on to it with the aid of two helpers.

2 Tense the blanket between two people with the third supporting the dog's back and manoeuvre it carefully into the car.

ACTION IN CASE OF COLLAPSE

1 Treat for shock Place the dog in a quiet, warm place and cover it with a blanket. Place a hot (not scalding) water bottle next to it to help minimize shock.
2 Check breathing If it is irregular or non-existent: ☐ loosen the collar ☐ open the mouth ☐ remove any foreign material, saliva, blood or vomit ☐ give artificial respiration (see right).
3 Check the pulse (see p.42). If you can't feel a pulse, try to feel a heartbeat by placing the fingertips on the left-hand side of the lower chest just behind the elbow. If you feel nothing, and the dog is unresponsive, give heart massage by vigorous squeezing of the left-hand side of the chest just behind the elbow – about one squeeze per second. (If the heart stops for more than three or four minutes, there may be irreversible brain damage.) Also give artificial respiration (see right).
4 Treat bleeding Staunch any heavy blood flow (see p.92).
5 Support broken bones (see p.93).
6 Contact the vet Arrange for an immediate veterinary examination.

ARTIFICIAL RESPIRATION

1 Check that the airway is clear, mouth open and clean, tongue forward.
2 Place both hands on the chest, over the rib area and push down firmly but gently to expel air from the lungs. Release the pressure immediately so that the chest expands and draws fresh air in.
3 Repeat at five-second intervals.

CONVULSIONS

The most usual cause is epilepsy (see p.76). This often starts with the dog being generally unsettled, then the fit/convulsions begin. Signs include: ☐ champing and chewing ☐ lips drawn back ☐ foaming at the mouth ☐ collapse and unconsciousness ☐ passing urine and faeces ☐ paddling of the legs.
Action
1 If the dog isn't a known epileptic, telephone the vet immediately.
2 Check that the dog is in a safe place, away from electric cables.
3 Make sure that the dog is comfortable; loosen its collar and cover it with a blanket if necessary. After this, avoid touching it until the fit is over.

4 Keep the room dark and quiet.
5 The fit shouldn't last more than five minutes. Once it is over, wipe the mouth and clean up any urine and faeces.
6 Let the dog have a drink but not much food until it is back to normal. Let it relax in quiet surroundings.
7 Follow the vet's instructions, going to the surgery or waiting for a visit.

DROWNING
Once you have the dog ashore, empty its lungs of water as quickly as possible.
Small dog Pick it up by the back legs and hold it upside down. Swing the dog round very carefully. A helper should then open its mouth and pump its chest.
Larger dog Pick it up behind the ribs, with one arm round the abdomen. Drape the dog over your shoulder while you open its mouth and pump its chest. *Don't* try to swing heavy dogs – you'll dislocate joints and tear ligaments.

HEATSTROKE
If left in an unventilated car in hot weather, a dog may suffer heatstroke. It will be in a variable state of collapse, panting heavily if conscious and frothing round the mouth.
Action
1 Clear froth from the mouth.
2 Douse the whole body with cold water.
3 Rush to the vet's surgery, where treatment will involve more cold water, stimulant drugs and cortisone.

FOREIGN BODY IN THE MOUTH
Restrain the dog (see p.82). If possible, open its mouth as if giving a pill (see p.85), and locate the foreign body. Remove it with your fingers or fine pliers if you can do this safely. If not, try the method described for emptying the lungs of water (see *Drowning*, left). If this fails, don't delay – contact a vet immediately.

FOREIGN BODY IN THE EYE
Stop the dog pawing its eye. If necessary, put a sock padded with cotton wool on each front paw. Restrain the dog (see p.82), and part the eyelids with finger and thumb to inspect the foreign body. If it is penetrating the eye, *don't touch it*, contact the vet immediately.

If the foreign body is sitting on the surface, try to remove it by irrigation (see p.69).

FOREIGN BODY IN THE THROAT
A stick or ball can lodge in a dog's throat or airway. If its larynx is blocked, the dog may have difficulty breathing and may die unless quick action is taken.

Try to remove the obstruction using the same method as for a drowning dog (see left). If this is unsuccessful, the object will have to be removed under anaesthetic by a vet.

POISONS
Fortunately poisoning is fairly rare in dogs, but they're less discriminating than cats and will eat a number of noxious substances. They may also lick off and swallow poisons that have contaminated their coat. Signs include: ☐ acute vomiting ☐ collapse ☐ violent muscular twitching ☐ fits ☐ weakness ☐ bleeding.
Action
1 Prevent further poison being swallowed. Wash off any on the coat.
2 Contact the vet immediately.
3 If you think you know what the dog has swallowed, take some with you to the vet, plus its container.

Don't waste time trying to treat the dog yourself – specific drugs may be needed. Your vet may tell you to make the dog vomit with an emetic. This is only worthwhile if the dog has eaten the poison during the last half hour. Suitable emetics are:
☐ washing soda (sodium carbonate) – a pea-sized piece given as a tablet, *not* caustic soda (sodium hydroxide)
☐ salt in warm water ☐ mustard in cold water.

Wounds and burns

The most common wounds sustained by dogs are bites from other dogs and cut feet. If you see blood on the coat, first locate the source. If this isn't obvious, feel for matted hair stuck to the skin.

Action

1 If necessary, clip away the hair so that you can see the wound clearly.
2 Control any bleeding (see below).
3 Bandage the wound if possible.
4 Treat for shock. Contact the vet.

TREATING "BURNS"

These are usually caused by spilling hot or caustic liquids on dogs. Other causes include: ☐ falling into a hot bath ☐ biting electric cables ☐ extreme cold.

Action

1 If an offending substance is still on the dog, wash it off with cold water.
2 Apply a greasy ointment such as petroleum jelly.
3 Treat for shock. Contact the vet.

CONTROLLING BLEEDING

To control bleeding, hold a pad over the injury and bind it tightly in place with a bandage. If bleeding continues, apply a pad and bandage to these pressure points:

Forelimb Brachial artery where it crosses the bone above the inner elbow.
Hind limb Femoral artery as it crosses the femur on the upper inner thigh.
Tail Coccygeal artery underneath tail.
Head and neck Push a finger firmly into the groove where the carotid artery meets the shoulder (this can't be done with a pad and bandage).

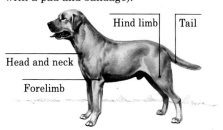

Hind limb | Tail

Head and neck

Forelimb

APPLYING BANDAGES

A bandage can protect an injury and keep it clean until it can be seen by a vet. You'll need an absorbent pad. Use lint, gauze, kitchen towel, even a clean handkerchief, but don't put cotton wool on a wound – it leaves fibres.

1 Try to close up the wound as much as possible and apply the pad to the site of the wound.

2 Wrap a crepe bandage round it four or five times, using other parts of the dog for anchorage.

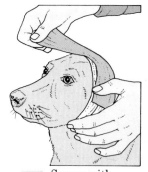

3 Secure with adhesive tape. *Never* use elastic bands – you could cut off the blood suppy.

DRESSING AN EYE WOUND

It is important that the surface of the eye doesn't dry out, so never bind a dry dressing over it. Use an absorbent pad soaked (but not dripping) in warm water. Secure the pad using a crepe bandage wound round the head with turns around the ear to keep it in place.

APPLYING A FOOT DRESSING

1 Insert pieces of cotton wool between the toes, then swathe the whole foot in cotton wool. This averts the danger of your stopping the circulation with a tight dressing.
2 Hold the padding in place with a bandage secured with adhesive tape.
3 Cover the dressing with a polythene bag, then a sock. Secure these with more tape above the "wrist".

DRESSING A TORSO WOUND

There are several ways of dealing with injuries to the chest or abdomen.
● A dressing pad can often be secured by bandaging the chest and one front leg.
● If this is tricky, cut a rectangle with "tapes" to tie over the back from a sheet.
● As a stop-gap, a towel or any other suitable piece of cloth can be wrapped round, then the ends twisted together over the back to draw it tight. Hold it in place until you reach the vet.

TREATING A SPRAIN

Dogs, particularly large ones, are prone to sprains (see p.78). Wrenched and damaged muscle also responds to the same treatment. The most important long-term treatment for severe sprains is weeks or even months of rest.
Action
1 Apply a cold compress immediately – cotton wool or cloth soaked in chilled water. Change this for a fresh compress every 20 minutes.
2 After a few hours change to a hot compress (soak in water as hot as the back of the hand will bear).
3 Support the limb with a crepe bandage.

APPLYING A SPLINT

Splints can be tricky, but if you suspect a fractured leg, it is well worth applying one if you can. You need a large roll of cotton wool, battens and a bandage. Try to arrange the limb in its normal extended position, and pad the site with cotton wool – the more the better.

1 To reduce swelling and assist repair, use the cotton wool as a bandage, winding it round the leg. Apply a layer twice as thick as the leg, as far up and down it as possible.

2 Once the leg is covered, lay two suitable solid battens on either side of the leg to act as splints and bind them firmly in place with a bandage. Contact a vet.

Index

ACKNOWLEDGEMENTS

Author's acknowledgements
I would first like to thank my colleague and friend Peter Scott for his tremendous contribution to this book; without him it could not have been written. Also the team at Dorling Kindersley, particularly Caroline Ollard and Derek Coombes for editing and design; their patience, expertise and dedication have been remarkable. Thanks are also due to Miss Horder, Librarian at the Royal college of Veterinary Surgeons – if this lady doesn't know a source of the most arcane information, it doesn't exist!

Dorling Kindersley would like to thank:
Iona McGlashan for design assistance, Richard Bird for the index, Bruce Fogle, Jenny Berry, Maxine Clark and Peter Olsen at the Portman Veterinary Clinic, Colin Tennant for training demonstrations and advice, Animal Fair of Kensington for loan of equipment, Susie McGowan, Mike Snaith and all at MS Filmsetting, Lucio Santoro, Chris Cope and Alison Graham.
and also:
Daisy, Tadpole, Gist, Kells puppy, Bicci, Heidi, Guffie and Polly

Picture research
Lesley Davy

Illustrators
Russell Barnett, Kuo Kang Chen

Photography
Jan Baldwin, Ian O'Leary

Jacket photography
Front: top and middle, Animal photography/Sally-Anne Thompson; bottom, Dave King; *Back:* top, Animal photography/Sally Anne Thompson; middle, Animals Unlimited/Paddy Cutts; bottom, Dave King

Typesetting
MS Filmsetting Limited, Frome, Somerset

Reproduction
Newsele SRL, Milan

Photographic credits
Animal Photography/Sally Anne Thompson: pp. 10, 11
Animals Unlimited/Paddy Cutts: p.17
Beaumont Animals Hospital, Royal Veterinary College, 79
Marc Henrie: pp. 2, 30
The Image Bank/Trevor Wood: p.7
NHPA/Lacz Lemoine: p.87
Panther Photographic International: p.1